Punjab,
Punjabis &
Punjabiyat

Also by Khushwant Singh

FICTION
Train to Pakistan
The Lost Victory
Delhi: A Novel
The Company of Women
Burial at Sea
The Sunset Club
The Portrait of a Lady: Collected Stories

NON-FICTION
Truth, Love & a Little Malice: An Autobiography
Delhi Through the Seasons
Indira Gandhi Returns
A History of the Sikhs
Ranjit Singh: Maharaja of Punjab

ANTHOLOGIES
The Freethinker's Prayer Book
Unforgettable Khushwant Singh: His Finest Fiction, Non-fiction, Poetry & Humour
Portrait of a Serial Killer: Uncollected Writings
Me, the Jokerman: Enthusiasms, Rants & Obsessions
Extraordinary Indians: A Book of Profiles

TRANSLATIONS
Land of Five Rivers
Umrao Jan Ada (with M. A. Husaini)
Shikwa and Jawab-i-Shikwa
Celebrating the Best of Urdu Poetry (with Kamna Prasad)

Punjab, Punjabis & Punjabiyat

REFLECTIONS ON A LAND AND ITS PEOPLE

KHUSHWANT SINGH

EDITED BY MALA DAYAL

ALEPH

ALEPH BOOK COMPANY
An independent publishing firm
promoted by *Rupa Publications India*

First published in India in 2018
by Aleph Book Company
7/16 Ansari Road, Daryaganj
New Delhi 110 002

ISBN: 978-93-87561-40-3

7 9 10 8 6

Printed in India

CONTENTS

INTRODUCTION

The pieces collected in this book are my father's best writings on Punjab, its land and people, history, religion, culture, literature and art. Together they give us a portrait of Punjab and Punjabiyat, as he saw it.

My father was born in Hadali in undivided Punjab. His love for his childhood home is expressed in an evocative autobiographical piece, 'Village in the Desert'. He returned to Hadali three times after Partition, and after he passed away in March 2014, a portion of his ashes was taken by train to Pakistan and buried there.

My father closely followed the political situation in Punjab and watched with dismay the growth of the Khalistan movement and the increasing influence of Bhindranwale. His anguish at the storming of the Golden Temple by the army was so great that he returned the Padma Bhushan awarded to him by the government. Many of his speeches in the Rajya Sabha, the diary he kept and his columns reflected his involvement and concerns about matters in Punjab.

Though a professed agnostic, my father identified himself as a Sikh. He was moved by the hymns of the Gurus, especially Guru Nanak's 'Bara Mah', which he lovingly translated. He was worried Sikhism would lose its distinctiveness as a faith and be absorbed by Hinduism.

His two-volume comprehensive and authoritative history of the Sikhs remains the most readable work on the subject. When he finished the second volume, he appended two words in Latin: Opus Exegii–my life's work has been done. He said: 'To write on Sikh religion and history was my life's ambition. Having done that I felt like one living on borrowed time, at peace with myself and the world. It would not bother me if I wrote nothing else.' Fortunately, not only did he continue writing—non-fiction and fiction—but with the years, his engaging prolific output made him a kind of icon.

The book ends with the profiles of some Punjabis, some well-known, others less so, but all of whom he admired to a lesser or a greater degree.

Since these pieces were written and published at different times, there is some repetition—this has been retained so that each article is complete in itself.

Mala Dayal
New Delhi

Khushwant Singh

PART I
PUNJAB AND PUNJABIYAT

THE LAND AND ITS PEOPLE

PUNJABI HOMELAND

Punjab has a geographical unity distinct from the neighbouring countries and the rest of India. It is shaped like a scalene triangle balanced on its sharpest angle. The shortest side is in the north and is composed of the massive Himalayas, which separate it from the Tibetan plateau. The western side is bounded by the river Indus from the point it enters the plains to another point 1,650 miles downstream, where it meets the confluence of Punjab's rivers at a place appropriately named Panjnad—the five streams. Westwards of the Indus runs a chain of rugged mountains, the Hindu Kush and the Sulaiman, pierced by several passes like the Khyber and the Bolan, which have served as inlets for the people of the countries which lie beyond, Afghanistan and Baluchistan. The eastern boundary of Punjab's triangle is not clearly marked, but from a point near Karnal where the Yamuna plunges southeastwards, a jagged line can be drawn up to Panjnad, which will demarcate the state from the rest of Hindustan and the Sindh desert. Punjab, except for the salt range in its centre, is an extensive plain sloping gently down from the mountains in the north and the west towards the desert in the south. Across this monotonously flat land flow six large rivers: the Indus, Jhelum, Chenab, Ravi, Beas, and Sutlej. In the intra-fluvial tracts or doabs between these rivers and in the western half of the tract between the Sutlej and the Yamuna, live people who speak Punjabi and describe themselves as the people of Punjab. The homeland of the vast majority of the Sikhs is in the doabs between the Chenab and the Yamuna.

3

THE NAME: PUNJAB

When the first settlers from Central Asia came to India, there were seven rivers in Punjab, so they named it Sapta Sindhva, the land of the seven seas. The Persians took the name from the Aryans and called it the Hafta Hindva. Sometime later, after the seventh river, the Sarasvati, had dried up, people began to exclude the Indus from the count (since it marked only the western boundary of the province) and renamed it after the remaining five rivers as Pentopotamia or the panj-ab, the land of the five waters.

CLIMATE AND LANDSCAPE

The climate of Punjab ranges from bracing cold in the winter to scorching heat in the summer. Extremes of temperature and the two monsoons produce a variety of seasons and a constantly changing landscape.

Spring is traditionally ushered in on Basant Panchami, which falls early in the month of February. It is Punjab's blossom time, when, in the words of Guru Nanak, 'all is seemly; the woodlands are in flower and loud with the humming of bumblebees'. The countryside is an expanse of mustard yellow, broken by solid squares of green sugarcane with its fluffy pampas plumes. If the winter monsoon has been good, a crop of wheat, barley, gram, oilseeds, and tobacco will cover the land with lush abundance. Peasants supplement the rain by canal water or, where there are no canals, by Persian wheels turned by bullocks or camels. Around the wells grow vegetables: carrots, radishes, cabbages, and cauliflower. Branches of jujube trees sag under the weight of their berries. In springtime, the sounds that pervade the countryside are the creaking of Persian wheels, the call of partridges, and the monotonous kooh kooh, of flour mills.

The sugarcane is cut, its juice squeezed out, boiled in large cauldrons, and solidified into dark brown cakes. The canary yellow of the mustard is replaced by newly sown cotton and the golden-brown of ripening wheat—and we know that spring has given way to summer.

Trees shed their leaves and after a short period of barrenness come into blossom. While the margosa is still strewing the earth with its brittle ochre leaves, the silk cotton, the coral and the flame of the forest

Khushwant Singh

burst into flowers of bright crimson, red, and orange. Even the thorny acacia, the commonest tree of Punjab, is covered with tiny pale pompoms. Persian wheels and the partridges are silent: instead there is the screaming of the koels in the mango groves and the crying of barbets. The wheat is cut and winnowed in the warm breeze. In the words of Guru Nanak: 'The sun scorches...the earth burns like an oven. The waters give up their vapours, yet it burns and scorches relentlessly.' The temperature rises to a fever heat.

The parched earth becomes an unending stretch of khaki with dust-devils spiralling across the wastes. Even the stolid peepal and the tamarisk are shorn of their leaves and the only green that meets the eye are bushes of camel-thorn, prickly cactus, and the ak—calotropis. The succession of hot days and shimmering mirages is occasionally broken by fierce storms which spread layers of dust and sand over everything. All through the torpid afternoons comes the call of the brainfever bird in a rising crescendo, peeooh peeooh. On moonlit nights one can see the wavering arrowhead formations of geese honking their way northwards to the snowy Himalayas.

The blazing inferno lasts from the end of April to the end of June. Then come the rains.

The monsoon makes a spectacular entry. It is heralded by the monsoon bird, the pied-crested cuckoo, which fills the dusty plains with its plaintive cries. The colourless grey sky suddenly fills with dense masses of black clouds. There are flashes of lightning and the earth shakes with the rumble of thunder. The first big drops of rain are swallowed by the dust and a heavenly fragrance rises from the earth. Then it comes in torrents, sheet upon sheet, and continues for several hours. Thereafter the skies are frequently overcast; clouds and sunshine contend for dominion; rainbows span the rain-washed landscape; and the setting sun fires the bulbous clouds in hues of red and purple. Two months of incessant downpour turn the land into a vast swamp. Rivers fill up and become a mass of swirling, muddy waters. Punjabis, who have to live through many months of intense heat every year, love the monsoon. It is the time for lovers' trysts and the reunion of families. Guru Nanak went into raptures over it: 'The season of the rains has come and my heart is full of joy...river and land are one expanse of water... The nights are dark. Frogs croak in contentment. Peacocks cry with joy. The papeeha calls peeooh peeooh. The fangs of serpents and the stings of mosquitoes are full of venom. The seas have burst their bounds in the ecstasy of fulfilment.' Life begins afresh. There are new leaves on many trees and grass covers the barren ground. Mangoes ripen. The clamour of the koels and the brainfever bird is drowned in the song and laughter of girls on swings in the mango groves.

By the time the monsoon is over, it is cool again. The dust has settled and the countryside is green once more. If the summer monsoon has been good—neither too sparse to create a drought nor too heavy to cause floods—all is well. A new crop of rice, millet, maize, indigo, and pulses of many kinds is sown. The peasants wind brightly coloured and starched turbans round their heads, put on waistcoats covered with mother-of-pearl buttons, tie bells round their ankles, and dance the bhangra to the beat of the drum. From October till Diwali in November there is a succession of fairs and festivals.

There is little rest for the peasant. Cotton is to be picked and the land ploughed again for sowing wheat and gram. Persian wheels begin to turn. The kooh, kooh of the flour mills is heard in every village. Partridges call in the wheat fields. And at night one hears the honking of geese on their way back to Punjab.

Once more it is wintertime. The starlit nights are cold and frosty, the days full of blue skies and sparkling sunshine. The mustard is in flower, the woodlands are loud with the humming of bumblebees, and all is seemly once again.

◆

Punjab is essentially a rural state made up of innumerable mud and brick villages built on the ruins of older villages. At one time most of them were fortified. Even today one comes across remains of baronial castles and ancient battlements that rise out of the rubble or the village dung heap. Until the fifteenth century, Punjab had only two important cities, Lahore, which was the seat of most governments, and Multan in the south, which had a busy market dealing with commerce coming up the rivers from Sindh and caravans from Baluchistan and Persia. There were also several towns like Rawalpindi, Jhelum, Wazirabad,

Gujarat, Gujranwala, Sheikhupura, Saidpur (now called Eminabad), Pak Pattan, Kasur, Sialkot, Ludhiana, and Sirhind, whose various fortunes rose and fell with those of their feudal overlords (or, as in the case of Pak Pattan, with the popularity of the religious order of which it was the centre). Nothing remains of the extensive forests which once covered large parts of Punjab. Up to the sixteenth century, there were jungles in the north where rhinoceros (and probably elephants) were found. In central Punjab, there was the notorious lakhi (the forest of a hundred thousand trees), which gave Sikh outlaws refuge from their oppressors. There were equally dense forests in the Jullundur Doab and one long belt of woodland stretching from Ludhiana to Karnal. Up to the middle of the nineteenth century, these forests teemed with wildlife: lions, tigers, leopards, panthers, bears, wolves, hyenas, wild boars, nilgai, and many varieties of deer. The flora and fauna survived the incursions of foreign armies but succumbed to the indiscriminate felling of trees and slaughter of game in the nineteenth and twentieth centuries. The desert with its camels and goats—the only animals that can thrive on cacti and thorny scrub—are a phenomenon of recent times.

THE PEOPLE OF PUNJAB
The ethnic pattern of Punjab has changed with every new conquest. At the time of the birth of Nanak (1469 CE), it was somewhat as follows:
     In the northwest stretching along both sides of the Indus were Pathans and Baluchis—the former on the upper and the latter on the lower reaches of the river. These people, like their neighbours (Gakkhars, Awans, Janjuas, and others who settled between the Indus and the Jhelum) were divided into innumerable warring tribes, jealously preserving their traditions and way of life but united in their fierce loyalty to the Islamic faith. On the northern fringe of the country in a narrow belt running along the foothills of the Himalayas were the domains of Hindu princes who had fled the plains in front of the Muslim onslaughts. In this sub-montane region intersected by mountain streams and deep ravines, made impassable by entangled bushes of lantana, vasica, and ipomoea, they built chains of forts which defended them from further inroads of Muslim invaders. Here they burnt incense to their gods and preserved their inegalitarian society

in which the Brahmins and Kshatriyas exploited the lesser castes. In the rest of Punjab, consisting of the vast champaign stretching to the Yamuna and beyond, the countryside was inhabited by Jats and Rajput agricultural tribes, the cities by the trading Banias, Mahajans, Suds and Aroras. In all cities, towns and villages there were the descendants of the aboriginals who were considered beyond the pale of the caste system, forced to do the dirtiest work and then condemned as untouchables. In addition to all these were nomadic tribes of gypsies wandering across the plains in their donkey caravans with their hunting dogs and herds of sheep and goats.

PUNJABI NATIONALISM

Punjab, being the main gateway into India, was fated to be the perpetual field of battle and the first home of all the conquerors. Few invaders, if any, brought wives with them, and most of those who settled in their conquered domains acquired local women. Thus the blood of many conquering races came to mingle, and many alien languages—Arabic, Persian, Pushto and Turkish—came to be spoken in the land. Thus, too, was the animism of the aboriginal subjected to the Vedantic, Jain and Buddhist religions of the Aryans, and to the Islamic faith of the Arabs, Turks, Mongols, Persians and Afghans. Out of this mixture of blood and speech were born Punjabi people and their language. There also grew a sense of expectancy that out of the many faiths of their ancestors would be born a new faith for the people of Punjab.

By the end of the fifteenth century, the different races who had come together in Punjab had lost the nostalgic memories of the lands of their birth and begun to develop an attachment to the land of their adoption. The chief factor in the growth of Punjabi consciousness was the evolution of one common tongue from a babel of languages. Although Punjabis were sharply divided into Muslims and Hindus, attempts had been made to bring about a rapprochement between the two faiths and a certain desire to live and let live had grown amongst the people. It was left to Guru Nanak and his nine successors to harness the spirit of tolerance and give it a positive content in the shape of Punjabi nationalism.

It is significant that the spirit of Punjabi nationalism first manifested itself in Majha, the heart of Punjab, and amongst a people who were deeply rooted in the soil. Although the founders and many of the leaders of the movement were not agriculturists, its backbone was the Jat peasantry of the central plains.

There are as many conjectures about the etymology of the word Jat as there are of the origin of the race. The Jats who made the northern plains of India their home, brought with them certain institutions, the most important being the panchayat, an elected body of five elders, to which they pledged their allegiance. Every Jat village was a small republic made up of people of kindred blood who were as conscious of absolute equality between themselves as they were of their superiority over men of other castes who earned their livelihood as weavers, potters, cobblers or scavengers. The relationship of a Jat village with the state was that of a semi-autonomous unit paying a fixed sum of revenue. Few governments tried to assert more authority, and those which did soon discovered that sending out armed militia against fortified villages was not very profitable. The Jat's spirit of freedom and equality refused to submit to Brahmanical Hinduism and in its turn drew the censure of the privileged Brahmins of the Gangetic plains who pronounced that 'no Aryan should stay in Punjab for even two days' because Punjabis refused to obey the priests. The upper-caste Hindu's denigration of the Jat did not in the least lower the Jat in his own eyes nor elevate the Brahmin or the Kshatriya in the Jat's estimation. On the contrary, he assumed a somewhat condescending attitude towards the Brahmin, whom he considered little better than a soothsayer or a beggar, and the Kshatriya, who disdained earning an honest living and was proud of being a mercenary. The Jat was born the worker and the warrior. He tilled his land with his sword girded round his waist. He fought more battles for the defence of his homestead than the Kshatriya for, unlike the martial Kshatriya, the Jat seldom fled from his village when the invaders came. And if the Jat was maltreated or if his women were molested by the conqueror on his way to Hindustan, he settled his score by looting the invaders' caravans on their return journey and freeing the women he was taking back. The Punjabi Jat developed an attitude of indifference to worldly possessions and an instinct for gambling with his life against the odds. At the same time he became conscious of his role in the defence of Hindustan. His brand of patriotism was at once hostile towards the foreigner and benign, even contemptuous, towards his own countrymen whose fate depended so much on his courage and fortitude.

PUNJAB AND HARYANA

Punjab and Haryana are the cradles of Indian civilization. Archaeologists have found implements made of quartzite fashioned over 300,000 years ago. Agricultural tools made of copper and bronze prove the existence of rural communities around 2500 BCE. Later excavations have unearthed whole cities that had marketplaces, marble baths, drainage systems and used intricately carved seals with hieroglyphics. The Indus Valley Civilization, as it came to be known, is amongst the oldest in the world. Relics of these olden times continue to be unearthed in different parts of both states.

Both Punjab and Haryana have more history than historical monuments, more facilities for tourists than places of touristic interest. Amritsar is Punjab's largest city and has Punjab's chief attraction for the tourist, its famed Golden Temple, the Sikhs holiest of holy shrines. At the foothills of the Himalayas is Anandpur where in 1699 the last of the Sikhs' ten Gurus, Gobind Singh, baptized the first five Sikhs into the militant fraternity he called the Khalsa or The Pure. Here, there are several temples as well as a fortress. Every spring at the Holi festival (Sikhs celebrate it a day later as Hola Mohalla) hundreds of thousands of Sikhs, notably Nihangs, descendants of two orders of warriors, gather and indulge in displays of mock combats on horseback and on foot.

An equally large complex of temples, palaces and forts is to be seen at Sirhind near Patiala. Besides these there are also remains of a Mughal and pre-Mughal city and the mausoleum of a famous divine, Hazrat Mujaddad-ud-din Altaf Sheikh Ahmed popularly known as Sirhindi to which Muslims from all over the world come to pay homage.

Haryana could rightly claim to be the birthplace of the most sacred religious scripture of Hinduism. At Kurukshetra was fought the famous eighteen-day battle of the Mahabharata between the Kurus and the Pandavas. On the eve of the battle, Sri Krishna, a reincarnation of God Vishnu, persuaded a very reluctant commander of the Pandava army to wage the battle for righteousness. This sermon known as the Bhagavad Gita emphasizes the moral principle of doing one's duty without consideration of reward, victory or defeat and is regarded as the essence of the teachings of the Vedas and the Upanishads. Kurukshetra is full of temples and tanks where pilgrims come to bathe on auspicious days.

It is through these two states that invaders from the northwest: Greeks, Turks, Mongols, Persians and Afghans entered India and where many battles which decided the fate of India were fought. Their sites are still marked with commemoration stones and mausolea of kings and commanders who fell in action. The most famous of these are at Panipat and Karnal in Haryana. Besides these, there are innumerable forts, too many to be named, scattered all over the countryside of the two states. As if to compensate for the paucity of truly great historical monuments, both states have developed wildlife sanctuaries along lakes, swamps and rivers with attractive tourist bungalows from where visitors can see a wide variety of wild fowl and herds of deer. Along all major highways are chains of milk bars and cafes named after birds of the region: Blue Jay, Dabchick, Magpie, Myna, Parakeet etc.

There are many things that Punjab and Haryana have in common. The most important of these is a common capital, Chandigarh. Since both states have laid claim to the city, it is administered by the central government as a union territory. However, in the same city reside governors of the two states, in the same office buildings on different floors are their separate secretaries and their respective high courts.

The city is beautifully located below the Shivalik range of hills. Two hill torrents were canalised to form a large lake with a most attractive boulevard along which the citizens take the morning and evening air and watch water fowl that have made Sukhna Lake a halting place on their migrations from Central Asia to India and back.

The city was designed by the famous French architect Le Corbusier, assisted by his cousin, Pierre Jeanneret and an Englishman and wife team, Maxwell Fry and Jane Drew. Corbusier himself designed most of its important public buildings including the Secretariat, the Legislative Assembly and the High Court. Many of these buildings are on 'stilts'. The style of architecture proved to be somewhat infectious as many private institutions and homes copied it.

Chandigarh is a very green city with a large variety of flowering trees specially chosen for their beauty by Dr M. S. Randhawa, a renowned civil servant and botanist. It also has an extensive rose garden named after the first Muslim President of India, Dr Zakir Hussain. There is also a 'park' with statuary made out of broken pieces of cups and saucers of which Chandigarhians are very proud.

WHO ARE THE SIKHS?

A Sikh has been defined by legislative enactment as one who believes in the ten Gurus and the Granth Sahib. The Sikhs themselves believe that the spirit of the founder, Guru Nanak, passed into his successors 'as one lamp lights another' and is today embodied in their scripture, the Granth Sahib (or Adi Granth).

Sikhs only number 14 million out of India's population of 700 million. Christians who number 20 million and Muslims who number over 70 million are in the reckoning of heads deserving of greater notice. Besides, Sikhs are usually considered a protestant and militant subsect of the Hindus and so denied the attention they deserve. It is no exaggeration to say that despite its small size, the Sikh community is today politically, economically, strategically and militarily more important than its under 2 per cent of the proportion of the population would warrant. It is not for nothing that a Sikh refers to himself as sava lakh—equal to a 125,000 or a fauj—an army.

There are four good reasons which make Sikhism a unique religion and the Sikhs a special community.

In the first place, of all the major religions of present-day India, Sikhism is the only one that is purely and entirely Indian by birth and development. Hinduism, though developed in India, very likely came along with the Sanskrit language. Islam likewise originated in Arabia and came to India with Muslim traders and conquerors. The same applies to Christianity and Zoroastrianism. Buddhism which was born in India was ousted from the land within a few centuries of its birth and few Buddhists remain in the country today. The resurgence of neo-Buddhism in recent years is as yet more a sociological than a religious phenomenon. Jainism, which was and is Indian, has so completely merged within the Hindu fold as to not be distinguishable from it. Fourteen million Sikhs represent the only major community of India who practise a faith that is purely and entirely of Indian origin.

The second reason is that Sikhism is perhaps the only religion in the world which could claim to be not only eclectic but also completely non-denominational. The sacred scripture of the Sikhs, the Adi Granth, contains not only the writings of the Sikh Gurus but also those of Hindu and Muslim saint-poets of all castes ranging from Brahmins to the untouchables from different parts of northern India. And the Adi Granth is to every Sikh the living embodiment of all his ten Gurus and the word of God spoken through them.

Third, the Sikh faith is a synthesis of the two major religions of India—Hinduism and Islam. Both these religions underwent considerable change because of their impact on each other. Movements towards a rapprochement were started from either end and the two blended in Sikhism which again, is the only living faith which could be described as both Muslim and Hindu. The Sikh Gurus did not leave the blending to chance but clothed it with a personality distinct from either of its two constituents. Sikhism is like the sangam where the two streams of Hinduism and Islam mingle to become a mighty river.

The fourth reason may appear more sociological than religious. The Sikhs are a unique example of a community that within a couple of centuries of its birth developed a faith, an outlook, a way of life and, according to some, even physical features so distinct from the two religions out of which they were born, so as to achieve the semblance of separate nationhood. And having become a nation, became the spearhead of a nationalist movement which gathered both parent communities within its fold, liberated its homeland from foreign oppression, turned the tide of invasion back into the homes of its traditional conquerors and extended Punjab's frontiers to Tibet, Afghanistan, Baluchistan and Sindh. The movement reached its climax under the Sikh ruler Maharaja Ranjit Singh and, having run its course, collapsed within ten years of his death. This aspect of the story of the Sikhs would at first sight seem purely political and not connected with their religion. That is not so. In the process of development, the last of the Sikh Gurus, Gobind Singh, invested his following with external symbols, chiefly unshorn hair and the beard which became an integral part of the Sikh way of life and the one factor distinguishing them from other communities, particularly the Hindus, from whom the vast majority were converted. Since the annexation of Punjab by the British in 1849 the Sikh community has had to wage a relentless struggle for survival as a separate community. The tendency to abandon external forms—unshorn hair and beard—has grown amongst men of the younger generation resulting in the lapse of an ever-increasing number of Sikhs into the Hindu fold. If the pace of this lapsing into Hinduism continues, we may witness the remarkable, and to most Sikhs of my way of thinking, tragic phenomenon of a people losing their distinctiveness and of a living faith consigning itself to the cold catacombs of history.

THE FOUNDING OF THE FAITH

The state of affairs in northern India preceding the birth of Nanak can be described in one word—chaotic. The reigning dynasty of the Lodis had begun to break up. In 1398, Timur had invaded India and devastated the plains up to Delhi. Even twenty years later, the country had not recovered from the blow, and a contemporary writer described the principal city of the province, Lahore, as a town 'in which no living thing except the owl of ill omen had its abode'. In Delhi itself, the authority of the Lodis did not extend beyond the city walls. There was lawlessness born out of uncertainty. From 1519 the Mughal Babur started his incursions. After invading India thrice, he finally came to establish his dynasty in 1526. But for the first few years his own authority and that of his son was repeatedly challenged, and insecurity continued. The common people suffered at the hands of marauders all claiming sovereignty for themselves. There is a legend that Nanak was himself imprisoned by Babur. Even if that is doubtful, he had something to say of the tyranny and repression. 'The age,' he said, 'is a knife. Kings are butchers. They dispense justice when their palms are filled... Wealth and beauty which afforded men pleasure have now become their bane... Decency and laws have vanished; falsehood stalks abroad... The vocation of priests is gone and the devil reads the marriage vows. Paeans of murder are sung. Blood is shed in place of saffron... Then came Babur to Hindustan. Death disguised as a Mughal made war on us. There was slaughter and lamentation. Did not Thou, O Lord, feel the pain?' It was veritably Kalyug, the dark age of the Hindus, when, in the words of Nanak, 'true men speak the truth and suffer for it; when penitents cannot perform penance; when he who repeats God's name meets obloquy'. It was a time when a person with a sensitive mind would begin to doubt the ultimate

17

triumph of right over wrong. He might seek escape in asceticism and solitary meditation; he might find the answer in either renouncing the world altogether as damned beyond redemption or coming back to it determined to redeem it.

Guru Nanak (1469–1539) was the son of a petty official living in a village some thirty miles from Lahore. He took to studying the Hindu and Muslim religions almost from his boyhood, and found himself constantly involved in argument and discussion with itinerant holy men. Although he married and had a family, the urge to find spiritual truth for himself proved too great. He temporarily abandoned his family and became a wanderer. He fasted, prayed and meditated. After many years of ascetic life, thought and contemplation, he felt qualified to convey his experiences to the people. He started with the simple statement: 'There is no Hindu, there is no Mussulman.' He took as his companions a low-caste Hindu and a Muslim musician, and the three went preaching from hamlet to hamlet. The Guru composed his sermons in verse, which his Muslim companion set to music and sang with the lute. His teachings fired the imagination of Punjab peasantry and a large number of followers gathered round him.

At first they were merely known as his disciples, in Sanskrit 'shish'. Sometime later these disciples became a homogeneous group whose faith was exclusively the teachings of Nanak. The 'shish' became the Sikh (corruption of the Sanskrit word).

Nanak was content to be a teacher. He made no claims to divinity or to kinship with God. 'I came in the course of nature,' he said, 'and according to God's order shall I depart.' He did not invest his writings with the garb of prophecy, nor his word with the sanctity of a 'message'. His teachings were essentially a crusade against cant and humbug in religion, and he had the courage to pattern his life according to his teachings. Two incidents in his life illustrate his approach. He went to bathe in the Ganga as all devout Hindus did. The Brahmins bathed and threw water towards the rising sun as an offering to their dead ancestors. Nanak faced the other way and threw water in the opposite direction. When questioned, he answered: 'I am watering my fields in Punjab. If you can throw water to the dead in heaven, it should be easier to send it to another place on earth.' On another

Khushwant Singh

occasion, he happened to fall asleep with his feet towards Mecca. An outraged priest woke him up and rudely drew his attention to the fact. Nanak simply said: 'If you think I show disrespect by having my feet towards the house of God, turn them in some other direction where God does not dwell.'

As he himself had combined his mission with the domestic obligations of a husband and father, he advocated a way of life which allowed for the discharge of civic obligations with the spiritual. He was strongly opposed to asceticism involving renunciation of the world:

> Religion lieth not in the patched coat the yogi wears
> Not in the staff he bears
> Nor in the ashes on his body.
> Religion lieth not in rings in the ears,
> Not in a shaven head
> Nor in the blowing of the conch shell.
> If thou must the path of true religion see
> Amongst the world's impurities, be of impurities free.

There are no entirely reliable accounts of Nanak's travels. By the time his biography came to be written, sixty or eighty years after his death, a mass of legend had been built around incidents of his life. He apparently travelled all over India and even as far as Persia or Arabia. His life was mostly spent in bringing Hindus and Muslims together. His personal success in this direction was remarkable. He was acclaimed by both communities. When he died, his body became a subject of dispute. The Muslims wanted to bury him, the Hindus to cremate him. Even to this day, he is regarded in Punjab as a symbol of harmony between the two major communities. A popular couplet describes him:

> Guru Nanak Shah Fakir
> Hindu Ka Guru, Mussulman Ka Pir.

> Guru Nanak, the King of Fakirs.
> To the Hindu a Guru, to the Mussulman a Pir.

The success of Nanak's mission in the short space of twenty to thirty years of teaching calls for comment. It was partly due to the fact that the ground had already been prepared for him by the Sufis and the Bhaktas. It was chiefly due to his own personality, which combined a gentle disposition with a stern and uncompromising attachment to principle; humility with a conviction of the greatness of his mission; and, above all, a kindly sense of humour, with which he got the people to see the ridiculous without being ridiculed. He made them come to him, not through a sense of remorse or repentance, but as to one who was at once warm-hearted and understanding—a friend and a father. He did not spare himself from his humour:

> When I am quiet, they say I have no knowledge
> When I speak, I talk too much they say;
> When I sit, they say an unwelcome guest has come to stay;
> When I depart, I have deserted my family and run away.
> When I bow, they say it is out of fear that I pray.
> Nothing can I do that in peace I may spend my time.
> Preserve Thy servant's honour now and hereafter,
> O Lord sublime.

The following that Nanak had created in his lifetime could at best be described as a group dissenting from both Hinduism and Islam. It was left to his successors to mould this group into a community with its own language and literature, religious beliefs and institutions, traditions and conventions.

THE SIKH CONCEPTION OF GOD AND GURU

The Sikhs believe in the unity of God and equate God with truth. Although Sikh monotheism has an abstract quality, there is nothing vague about it. The preamble to the morning prayer Japji, which is recited as an introduction to all religious ceremonies and is known as the Mool Mantra, the basic belief, states:

> There is one God.
> He is the supreme truth.
> He, the creator,
> Is without fear and without hate.
> He, the omnipresent,
> Pervades the universe.
> He is not born,
> Nor does He die to be born again.
>
> Before time itself
> There was truth.
> When time began to run its course
> He was the truth.
> Even now, He is the truth.
> Evermore shall truth prevail.
> (Guru Nanak)

There was a change of emphasis in the conception of God in the writing of the tenth Guru, Gobind Singh. To him, although God was still one, the aspect of timelessness and of the power to destroy was more important than the creative. 'I performed great austerities and worshipped great death,' he wrote. Gobind Singh elevated death and time to the status of God. He enjoined respect, if not worship, for steel (sarb loh) as the symbol of destruction. He described God as Akal Purukh (timeless):

21

Time is the only God,
The primal and the final,
The creator and the destroyer.
How can words describe Him?

An excellent example of his notion of God is in one of his compositions
translated by Macauliffe:

Eternal God,
Thou art our shield,
The dagger, knife, the sword we wield.
To us protector there is given
The timeless, deathless, Lord of Heaven,
To us all-steel's unvanquished might,
To us all-time's resistless flight,
But chiefly Thou, protector brave,
All-steel, wilt Thine own servant save.

The attitude of the two Gurus, which seems at first sight to be
divergent, is not really so. The basic factors in the conception of
God were oneness and truth. Other attributes, such as omnipresence,
omniscience, formlessness, timelessness, and the power to destroy (evil),
were complementary and also referred to frequently by Nanak. Guru
Gobind gave them prominence by constant emphasis.

Although God has no form (nirankar) or substance and is beyond
human comprehension, by righteous living one can invoke His grace.
In the first verse of the morning prayer, Nanak said:

Not by thought alone
Can He be known,
Though one think a hundred thousand times.
Not in solemn silence,
Nor in deep meditation.
Though fasting yields an abundance of virtue,
It cannot appease the hunger for truth.
No, by none of these
Nor by a hundred thousand other devices
Can God be reached.

How then shall the Truth be known?
How the veil of false illusion torn?
O Nanak: thus runneth the writ divine,
The righteous path let it be Thine.

Sikh emphasis on action as a means to salvation is a departure from the predestination, and consequent passiveness, of the Hindu belief. Nanak, fond of using rural similes, wrote:

As a team of oxen are we driven
By the ploughman, our teacher.
By the furrows made are thus writ
Our actions—on the earth, our paper.
The sweat of labour is as beads
Falling by the ploughman as seeds sown,
We reap according to our measure
Some for ourselves to keep, some to others give.
O Nanak, this is the way to truly live.

And again:

If thou wouldst the fruits of salvation cultivate
And let the love of the Lord in thy heart germinate,
Thy body be as the fallow land
Where in thy heart the Farmer sows His seeds
Of righteous action and good deeds,
Then with the name of God irrigate.

Although Sikhism accepts the Hindu theory of karma and life hereafter, it escapes the maze in which life, death and rebirth go on as if it were independent of human volition. The Sikh religion states categorically that the first form given to life is the human ('Thou has the body of man, now is thy turn to meet God'—Guru Arjun). Human actions determine the subsequent forms of life to be assumed after death. It also believes that by righteous living and grace, it is possible to escape the vicious circle of life and death and attain salvation:

He who made the night and day,
The days of the week and the seasons,

He who made the breezes blow, the waters run,
The fires and the lower regions,
Made the earth—the temple of law.

He who made creatures of diverse kinds
With a multitude of names,
Made this the law—
By thought and deed be judged forsooth
For God is true and dispenses truth.
There the elect His court adorn,
And God Himself their actions honours.
There are sorted deeds that were done and bore fruit
From those that to action could never ripen.
This, O Nanak, shall hereafter happen.
(Guru Nanak)

The Sikh religion, believing as it does in the unity and formlessness of God, expressly forbids, in no uncertain terms, the worship of idols and emblems:

They who worship strange gods
Cursed shall be their lives, cursed their habitations.
Poison shall be their food—each morsel,
Poisoned too shall be their garments.
In life for them is misery,
In life hereafter, hell.
(Amar Das, third Guru)
Some worship stones and on their heads bear them,
Some the phallus strung in necklaces wear its emblem.
Some behold their God in the south, some to the west bow their head.
Some worship images, others busy praying to the dead.
The world is thus bound in false ritual
And God's secret is still unread.
(Guru Gobind)

Guru Nanak, while attending the evening service at a Hindu temple

where a salver full of small oil lamps and incense was being waved in front
of the idol before it was laid to rest for the night, composed this verse:

The firmament is Thy salver,
The sun and moon Thy lamps,
The galaxy of stars
Are as pearls scattered.
The woods of sandal are Thine incense,
The forests Thy flowers,
But what worship is this
O Destroyer of Fear?

THE GURU OR THE TEACHER

God being an abstraction, godliness is conceived more as an attribute
than a concrete something which can be acquired by a person or a thing.
The way of acquiring godliness or salvation is to obey the will of God.
The means of ascertaining God's will are, as in other theological systems,
unspecified and subject to human speculation. They are largely rules
of moral conduct, which are the basis of human society. Sikh religion
advocates association with men of religion for guidance. Hence the
importance of the Guru or the teacher and institution of discipleship.

The Sikhs do not worship human beings as incarnations of God.
The Sikh Gurus themselves insisted that they were human like other
human beings and were on no account to be worshipped. Guru Nanak
constantly referred to himself as the slave and servant of God. Guru
Gobind Singh, who was the author of most of the Sikh practice and
ritual, was conscious of the danger of having divinity imposed on him
by his followers. He explained his mission in life:

For though my thoughts were lost in prayer
At the feet of Almighty God,
I was ordained to establish a sect and lay down its rules.
But whosoever regards me as Lord
Shall be damned and destroyed.

I am—and of this let there be no doubt—
I am but the slave of God, as other men are,

A beholder of the wonders of creation.

In another passage, he refuted the claims to divinity and reincarnation made by others:

> God has no friends nor enemies.
> He needs no hallelujahs nor cares about curses.
> Being the first and timeless
> How could He manifest Himself through those
> Who are born and die?

Godliness being the aim of human endeavour, the lives and teachings of the Gurus are looked upon as aids towards attainment. 'On meeting a true Guru doubt is dispelled and wanderings of the mind restrained.' (Guru Nanak)

THE ROOTS OF SIKHISM

Sikhism was, and is, a pacifist creed started by Guru Nanak and developed by four succeeding Gurus whose writings were compiled in an anthology, the Adi Granth, by the fifth Guru, Arjun, around 1600 CE. The Adi Granth comprises over 6,000 hymns composed by five Gurus (mainly those of the compiler Guru Arjun) and includes compositions of Hindu and Muslim saints as well as some bards.

In the final version, the one compiled by Guru Gobind Singh, he inserted hymns composed by his father, Guru Tegh Bahadur. Guru Gobind compiled an anthology of his own, the Dasam Granth. While the Adi (first) Granth is essentially a distillation of the Vedanta in Punjabi, the Dasam (tenth) Granth is a compilation of tales of valour of Hindu goddesses, some composed by the Guru himself, others by the bards of his court. It is not accorded the same status as the Adi Granth. Thus we have two parallel scriptures, one extolling the virtues of peaceful submission, the other of combating oppression with force.

The martyrdom of two Gurus changed the course of Sikh history. Guru Arjun succumbed to torture in Lahore jail in 1606; his son and sixth Guru, Har Gobind, took up arms. Tegh Bahadur was executed in Delhi in 1675; his son Gobind Rai (later Singh) converted a sizeable chunk of hitherto peace-loving Sikhs into the militant fraternity called the Khalsa or the 'pure'.

As a consequence of these historic changes, we have several brands of Sikhs. There are Hindus who believe in Sikhism, visit gurdwaras, have a Granth Sahib in their homes and perform rituals according to Sikh rites. A large section of them are from Sindh, mainly Amils. Then there are Sahajdharis (slow adopters) who don't wear the external forms of the Khalsa—the unshorn hair and beard. The majority of Sikhs are Khalsa who undergo baptism (pahul), take vows to observe the five Ks—kesh, kangha, kachha, karha and kirpan—and add the suffix Singh, and if female, Kaur, to their names.

Those Khalsa who cut off their hair and shave their beards are regarded as patits (renegades) but still see themselves as Sikhs. The matter becomes more complex as, while all the above categories of Sikhs revere only ten Gurus and the Granth Sahib as their living embodiment, there are two sects—Nirankaris and Namdharis—who have living Gurus but nevertheless describe themselves as Sikhs.

Transition from one Sikh sect to the other, indeed from Hinduism to Sikhism, is without many hassles. Inter-marriage is not uncommon. The relationship between Hindus and Sikhs has always been roti-beti ka rishta (breaking bread together and giving daughters in marriage) or nauh-maas da rishta (as fingernail is to the flesh). In this situation, the Khalsa find themselves losing ground, as an increasing number of their youth cut their hair and shave their beards to become no different from Hindus believing in Sikhism, while the number of Hindus accepting baptism to become Khalsa is becoming rarer.

When the Khalsa was in the ascendant politically, their numbers rose steadily. After they lost their kingdom in 1849, their population began to decline. Fortunately for them, the British came to their aid by giving them preferential treatment in services like the army and the police; separate electorates; and reservation of seats in elected bodies like municipalities, legislatures and the central assembly. With Independence, such privileges were abolished and the economic benefits that came with being Khalsa disappeared.

In growing numbers, young Sikhs began to abandon the external symbols of the Khalsa. This was more noticeable amongst Sikhs settled in foreign countries. Wherever they were in large numbers and formed compact social groups—as in some East African countries and Singapore—social pressures kept the younger generation from reneging on their ancestral faith; where they were scattered in small numbers as in England, Canada and the US, a second generation emigrant conforming to Khalsa traditions became a rarity. The same phenomenon is visible amongst the educated elite who live in Indian cities and are exposed to Western influences. Young Sikh boys question the necessity of keeping long hair and growing beards to be religious.

The only rational answer is that it gives them a sense of belonging to the Khalsa Panth. Many don't find that convincing enough and become like Hindus performing Sikh rituals and prayer. The real danger to the Khalsa has always been, as it is today, the absorptive capacity of Hinduism. An English scholar correctly described it as the boa constrictor of the Indian jungles: it can swallow religions which come in contact with it, with a special taste for its own offspring.

The real challenge facing the Khalsa Panth will be to find ways and means to arrest, possibly reverse, the process of disintegration. Perhaps the most important issue to be considered by scholars of Sikh theology will be to convince people that there is a continuous and unbroken line between the teachings of Guru Nanak and the first five Gurus enshrined in the Adi Granth and the militant tradition begun by the sixth Guru and brought to culmination by the tenth and last Guru, Gobind Singh, with the establishment of the Khalsa Panth.

The roots of Sikhism lie deep in the Bhakti form of Hinduism. Guru Nanak picked what he felt were its salient features: belief in one God who is undefinable, unborn, immortal, omniscient, all-pervading and the epitome of truth; belief in the institution of the Guru as the guide in matters spiritual; unity of mankind without the distinction of caste; rejection of idol worship and meaningless ritual; sanctity of the sangat (congregation), which was expected to break bread together at the Guru ka langar; the gentle way of sahaj to approach God while fulfilling domestic obligations; hymn singing (kirtan); emphasis on work as a moral obligation. A slogan ascribed to Guru Nanak is 'kirat karo, vand chhako, naam japo' (work, share what you earn, take the name of the Lord). There's little doubt that Nanak felt he had a new message that needed to be conveyed, which is why he nominated his closest disciple Angad to be his successor in preference to his two sons. Angad, likewise, nominated his disciple Amar Das to succeed him. Thereafter, guruship remained amongst members of the same family, the Sodhis.

The compilation of the Adi Granth was a landmark in the evolution of Sikhism. Though an eclectic work with compositions of Hindu and Muslim saints, it echoes the Vedanta through most of its nearly 6,000 hymns. There is a new breed of Sikh scholars who bend backwards to prove Sikhism has taken little or nothing from Hinduism. All they need to be told is that of the 15,028 names of God that appear in the Adi Granth, Hari occurs over 8,000 times, Ram 2,533 times, followed by Prabhu, Gopal Govind, Prabhram and other Hindu nomenclature for the Divine. The purely Sikh coinage 'Wahe Guru' appears only sixteen times.

There can be little doubt that the martyrdom of Guru Arjun in 1606 resulted in a radical change in the community's outlook. Though its creed remained wedded to the Adi Granth, it was ready to defend itself by the use of arms. Guru Arjun's son, the sixth Guru, Har Gobind, raised a cavalry of horsemen. He built the Akal Takht facing the Harmandir Sahib (Golden Temple) as the seat of temporal power and came to be designated Miri Piri Da Malik (lord of temporal and spiritual power). For some years he was imprisoned in Gwalior Fort. The final transition came after the execution of the ninth Guru, Tegh Bahadur, in 1675. His son, Guru Gobind, justified the transition in a letter, *Zafarnama*, believed to have been addressed to Emperor Aurangzeb: 'When all other means have failed it is righteous to draw the sword'. Guru Gobind's concept of God underwent a martial metamorphosis. In his ode to Goddess Chandi, Guru Gobind asked Lord Shiva to grant him the most fitting end to a warrior's life:

> O Lord, these boons of Thee I ask,
> Let me never shun a righteous task,
> Let me be fearless when I go to battle,
> Give me faith that victory will be mine,
> Give me power to sing Thy praise,
> And when comes the time to end my life,
> Let me fall in mighty strife.

Though not very successful in the campaigns he fought, he fired his followers with martial fervour. 'I will teach the sparrow to hunt the hawk, one man to fight 125,000 (sava lakh).' He made the downtrodden feel they were God's chosen people—Wahe Guru ji da Khalsa—and would be ever victorious—Wahe Guru ji di Fateh.

The Guru succeeded in creating a new breed of intrepid warriors imbued with a do-or-die spirit. Within a few years of his death, disciple

Banda Bairagi overran the region around Sirhind and laid to waste large domains of the Mughal kingdom. Even after the capture and execution of hundreds of Banda's followers, bands of Sikh horsemen harried Nadir Shah's forces and forced his successor Ahmed Shah Abdali, who blew up the Harmandir Sahib twice, to retreat. When Sikhs became rulers of Punjab, Maharaja Ranjit Singh realized the value of having troops of Nihangs whom he threw into battles against Ghazis waging jihad against him. The determination never to give in came to be deeply rooted in the Sikh psyche; even in adversity they were exhorted to remain in buoyant spirits—charhdi kala. With it came the conviction that destiny was in their hands. At the end of each congregational prayer, comes the chant 'Raj Karega Khalsa' (the Khalsa will rule). No one will be able to resist them. Those who confront them will be routed. Those who seek their protection will be saved.

THE BUILDING OF THE SIKH CHURCH

ANGAD (1504–1552)

Lehna had been a devout Hindu before he met Nanak. At the very first meeting he fell under the spell of the Guru's words and abandoned the worship of his gods and his business, to devote himself to the service of the Sikh community at Kartarpur. Twice Nanak persuaded him to return to his family at Khadur, but both times he came back. His devotion convinced the Guru that Lehna would make a better leader than either of his own sons. An additional factor in preferring Lehna was the fact that he had a sizeable following of his own which he was gradually bringing into the Sikh fold. To forestall subsequent opposition from his sons, Nanak expressed his preference for Lehna in public: 'Thou art Angad, a part of my body.' Long before his death he had one of his chief disciples, Bhai Buddha, daub Angad's forehead with saffron and proclaim him as the second Guru.

Sri Chand was not an ambitious man. Nevertheless, since he was the elder son of the Guru and a man of pious habits, there were many who believed that Nanak's place should go to him. They refused to accept Angad's (as Lehna came to be known) succession and began to create difficulties. On the advice of Nanak, Angad 'left Kartarpur and went and lit the Guru's lamp in Khadur', where his wife and children were living.

Angad was Guru for thirteen years (1539–52). By his tact and humility he was able to prevent the schism between his Sikhs and Sri Chand's followers, who came to be known as Udasis (from 'Udas', one who has renounced the world). In his own quiet way he filled in the brickwork of the edifice whose scaffolding had been erected by Nanak. As the number of disciples increased, the expenses of the langar went up. Angad opened more centres and organized a regular system of collecting offerings to meet their expenses. He had copies made of Nanak's hymns and supplied one to each centre. These copies were made in a script which until then had no precise alphabet of its own. Angad took the thirty-five letters of the acrostic composed by Nanak, selected the appropriate letters from other scripts in use in northern India, and called the new script Gurmukhi (from the mouth of the Guru). This step had far-reaching results. Angad's compilation became the nucleus of the sacred writings of the Sikhs. It gave the Sikhs a written language distinct from the written language of the Hindus or the Mussalmans and thus fostered a sense of their being a separate people.

Angad was very keen on physical fitness. He ordered his followers to take part in drill and competitive games after the morning service. Every community centre had a wrestling arena attached to it. He started a tradition which made it easy for his successors to raise troops of able-bodied men from amongst the disciples.

Angad had two sons but he chose a seventy-three-year-old disciple, Amar Das, a Khatri of the Bhalla sub-caste to succeed him as the third guru.

AMAR DAS (1479–1574)
Amar Das had been a devout Hindu enjoying a reputation for kindliness and piety long before his conversion to Sikhism. He showed great devotion in forwarding the work that Nanak and Angad had begun. He made the langar an integral institution of the Sikh church by insisting that anyone who wanted to see him had first to accept his hospitality by eating with the disciples. The number of the Guru's visitors increased so much that Goindwal, where he lived, grew from an insignificant hamlet to a sizeable town. Amongst the people who visited him was Emperor Akbar, who was so impressed with the way of life at Goindwal that he assigned the revenues of several villages to the Guru's daughter, Bhani, as a marriage gift. Royal patronage gave further momentum to Nanak's movement.

Amar Das felt that he alone could not minister to the needs of the thousands of converts who wanted guidance. He increased the number of parishes or manjis to twenty-two and appointed agents (masands) who were fully conversant with the doctrines of the faith, to organize worship and the collection of offerings. He had more copies made of the hymns of Nanak and Angad and added to them his own compositions and those of the Hindu Bhaktas whose teachings were in conformity with those of Nanak. Since this anthology was in Punjabi, it gained enormous popularity amongst the masses, who did not understand either the Sanskrit texts of the Hindus or the Arabic of the Muslims. It reduced the importance of the Brahmin priests, who had maintained a strict monopoly over the knowledge of the sacred texts, and that of the mullahs, who alone could interpret the Quran.

Amar Das introduced many innovations which tended to break the close affiliations of the Sikhs with the Hindus. He sanctified a well alongside the temple at Goindwal and fixed the first of the Hindu month of Baisakh, which fell late in spring, as the day for the annual gathering of Sikhs. He also introduced new forms of ceremonial for births and deaths, in which the recitation of hymns of the Gurus replaced the chanting of Sanskrit slokas. He tried to do away with the practice of purdah (seclusion of women), advocated monogamy, encouraged inter-caste alliances and remarriage of widows. He strictly forbade the practice of sati—the burning of widows on the funeral pyres of their husbands.

These measures aroused the hostility of the Brahmins, who saw the size of their flock and their incomes diminishing. They began to persecute the Sikhs and, when their own resources failed, reported Amar Das to the emperor. When Akbar refused to take action against the Guru, they bribed local officials to harass the Sikhs. This was the beginning of the oppression of the Sikhs, which subsequently compelled them to take up arms, and the first break with Hindu social polity.

Amar Das's twenty-two years of ministry were a definite phase in the building of the Sikh church. He was a popular teacher because his sermons were simple and direct. 'Do good to others by giving good advice, by setting a good example, and by always having the welfare of mankind in your heart,' he said. Amar Das's work is applauded in the Adi Granth in the following words:

He made Divine Knowledge his steed and Chastity his saddle.
On the bar of truth he strung the arrow of God's praise.
In age of utter darkness, he rose like the Sun.
He sowed the seed of and reaped its fruit.

Amar Das lived to the age of ninety-five. He did not consider any of his sons fit to succeed him and chose instead his son-in-law, Ram Das, a Khatri of the Sodhi sub-caste who had been living with him for some years.

RAM DAS (1534–1581)

Ram Das had spent the better part of his forty years in the service of the community when he was called upon to become its leader. He had looked after the administration of the parishes and had represented Amar Das at the Mughal court. He had a tank dug at the site granted to his wife by Emperor Akbar. When he became Guru, he moved from Goindwal to the neighbourhood of the tank and started building a town around it. The town, which was destined to become the religious capital of the Sikhs, came to be known after him as Guru ka Chak, Chak Ram Das, or Ram Das Pura. He invited tradesmen to set up business in the town, and with the revenues so obtained he was able to expand his activities to distant parts of India. The most distinguished of his missionaries was Bhai Gurdas, who spent some years preaching in Agra.

Like his predecessors, Ram Das composed hymns which were later incorporated in the collection of sacred writings.

Ram Das had three sons, of whom he considered the youngest, Arjun Mal, the most suited to succeed him. This, as was to be expected, aroused the ire of the eldest, Prithi Chand. Nevertheless, when Ram Das felt his end near, he had the ageing Bhai Buddha invest Arjun Mal as the fifth Guru. Ram Das expressed the hope that 'As one lamp is lighted from another, so the Guru's spirit will pass into him and will dispel the darkness in the world.'

ARJUN (1563–1606)

Arjun's path, like that of his three predecessors, was full of pitfalls. As soon as his succession was proclaimed, his elder brother, Prithi Chand, turned violently hostile. Arjun was fortunate in having the loyal support of the venerable Buddha and Bhai Gurdas in thwarting the machinations of Prithi Chand and preventing a schism in the community.

Arjun's first task was to complete the building of a temple in Cak Ram Das. He invited the Muslim divine Mian Mir of Lahore to lay the foundation stone of the Harmandir, the temple of God. Instead of building the shrine on a high plinth as was the Hindu custom, Arjun had it built on a level lower than the surrounding land, so that the worshippers would have to go down the steps to enter it. And, unlike Hindu temples, which had only one entrance, Arjun had the Harmandir open on all four sides. These architectural features were intended to be symbolic of the new faith, which required the lowest to go even lower and whose doors were ever open to all who wished to enter.

Arjun had to raise money for the building of the temple. All Sikhs were asked to donate a tenth of their income (dasvandh) in the name of the Guru. The masands were instructed to come to Cak Ram Das every first of Baisakh to render accounts and bring with them as many Sikhs as could conveniently accompany them. In this way a central finance pool was created for the construction of the temple, as well as for starting other communal projects. The modest town grew into the premier commercial city of the province. After the temple was completed and the tank filled with water, it was given a new name, Amrit-sar (Pool of Nectar). What Benares was to the Hindus and Mecca to the Muslims, Amritsar became to the Sikhs: their most important place of pilgrimage.

Arjun undertook a tour of the neighbouring country. In 1590 he had another tank dug at a place about eleven miles south of Amritsar, which he blessed as Taran Taran (Pool of Salvation). It soon earned a reputation for having healing properties and Taran Taran became another place of pilgrimage, particularly for those afflicted with leprosy. A large temple and a leprosarium were built near the tank.

From Taran Taran, Arjun went to the Jullundur Doab and raised a third town called Kartarpur. From Kartarpur he went to Lahore and from there to the river Beas, on whose banks he built yet another town which he named after his son, Hargobind, as Sri Hargobindpur. In five years of travelling in central Punjab, Arjun brought into his fold thousands of Jats of the Majha country, the sturdiest peasants of Punjab.

Arjun returned to Amritsar in 1595 and discovered that Prithi Chand had not been idle in forwarding his pretensions. He had begun to compile an anthology of 'sacred' writings in which he was inserting compositions of his own. Arjun realized the danger of a spurious scripture gaining currency. He abandoned his other pursuits in order to make an authentic compilation of the writings of his predecessors. He had his father's hymns with him. He persuaded Mohan (son of Guru Amar Das) to give him the collection of the writings of the first three Gurus. He sent disciples to scour the country for copies that might have been made. He welcomed contributions from different sects of Hindus and Muslims for consideration. Then he installed himself by the Ramsar tank, which was well removed from the noise and bustle of the bazaars of Amritsar, and devoted himself entirely to the task. The selection was made by the Guru (his own contribution being the largest) and taken down by Bhai Gurdas.

While the Guru was busy with his work, a report was sent to Akbar that Arjun's sacred anthology had passages vilifying Islam. On his way north, the emperor stopped en route and asked to see the compilation. Bhai Buddha and Gurdas brought a copy of the existent manuscript and read some of the hymns to Akbar. The emperor, his fears dispelled, made an offering of fifty-one gold mohurs to the sacred book and gave robes of honour to the two disciples and sent one for Guru Arjun. At the Guru's request, he also remitted the annual revenue of the district to ameliorate the condition of the peasants, who had been hard hit by the failure of the monsoon.

In August 1604 the work was completed and the Granth Sahib, the holy volume, was formally installed in the temple at Amritsar. Bhai Buddha was appointed the first reader or granthi. The Granth reflected the faith of Nanak in its entirety. Apart from the writings of the Gurus, it contained a selection of the compositions of the poet-saints from all parts of northern India, both Muslim and Hindu, of all castes, including the 'untouchables'. Its hymns were of a high poetic order, its language intelligible to the illiterate peasant, its ethics simple and direct. The Granth became the most powerful factor in spreading the teachings of the Gurus amongst the masses. In the last hymn before writing the finis, Arjun made the following claim for his anthology: 'In this vessel you will find three things—truth, peace and contemplation; in this too the nectar that is the Name of the Master which is the uplifter of all mankind.'

Emperor Akbar was impressed by the Guru's work, for it echoed some of the beliefs he held sacred. On one occasion he stopped at Goindwal for the express purpose of meeting the Guru. The emperor's admiration was an important factor in building Sikh fortunes. During the seven years between the emperor's first visit to Goindwal and his death in 1606, the number of Sikhs increased and trade thrived in the four towns Arjun had built. He became a leader of national importance, and his church grew rich and powerful. The Guru began to be addressed as the Sacha Padshah (the true emperor).

The death of Akbar brought a sudden reversal in the policy of the state towards the Sikhs. The new emperor, Jahangir, disapproved of the growing popularity of Guru Arjun. In his diary he wrote: 'At last when Khusrau [his son] passed along this road this insignificant fellow [Arjun] proposed to wait upon him. Khusrau happened to halt at the place where he was, and he came out and did homage to him. He behaved to Khusrau in certain special ways and made on his forehead a finger mark in saffron, which the Indians call qasqa and is considered to be propitious. So many of the simple-minded Hindus, nay, many foolish Muslims too, had been fascinated by his ways and teachings. He was noised about as a religious and worldly leader. They called him Guru, and from all directions crowds of fools would come to him and express great devotion to him. This busy traffic had been carried on for three or four generations. For years the thought had been presenting itself to my mind that either I should put an end to this false traffic, or he should be brought into the fold of Islam.'

Jahangir found an excuse to put an end to the 'false traffic' within a few months of his accession. Khusrau rebelled against his father and sought the Guru's assistance and blessing. Arjun received the prince, as indeed he would have even if the visitor had not been of royal blood. He did not give Khusrau any assistance beyond perhaps wishing him well. Nevertheless, after the rebellion had been suppressed and Khusrau apprehended, Jahangir wreaked terrible vengeance on the people he suspected of having helped his son. Arjun was heavily fined and, on his refusal to admit the charge of treason or pay the fine, was arrested and sentenced to death. Jahangir wrote: 'I fully knew his heresies, and I ordered that he should be brought into my presence, that his houses and children be made over to Murtaza Khan, that his property be confiscated, and that he should be put to death with torture.'

The Guru was taken to Lahore. Amongst his tormentors was a Hindu banker whose daughter's hand Arjun had refused to accept for his son. Amongst those who tried in vain to intercede on his behalf was the Muslim divine Mian Mir. Arjun was tortured until he was unable to stand any more. He sent word to his son, Hargobind, who was only eleven years old, to ask Bhai Buddha to install him as the sixth guru and to assume the ministry of the community.

During one of the intermissions in the torture, Arjun was allowed to wash himself in the Ravi, which ran alongside the prison. On 30 May 1606, the Guru entered the stream. The impact of the cold water proved too much for his fevered body, and the current bore him beyond the reach of his tormentors.

Arjun was an unusually gifted and prolific writer. His lines were resplendent with bejewelled phrases and his hymns full of haunting melody. His most popular composition was the *Sukhmani* (the Psalm of Peace), in which he wrote: 'Of all creeds the sovereign creed is to pray to God and do a goodly deed.'

Arjun had become the most quoted poet of Punjab. His songs were on the people's lips and while they eagerly awaited his voice, Jahangir brutally silenced it forever. In the twenty-five years of Arjun's ministry, the seed sown by Nanak blossomed into its fullness. Nanak's teaching, which was embodied in the hymns of his successors, had been compiled in the Granth. Nanak's way had become the way of life of communities of Sikhs scattered all over northern India. The Sikhs had become conscious of the fact that they were now neither Hindus nor Muslims but formed a third community of their own.

This feeling was expressed by Arjun in many of his writings:

I do not keep the Hindu fast, nor the Muslim Ramzan.
I serve Him alone who is my refuge.
I serve the One Master, who is also Allah.
I have broken with the Hindu and the Muslim.
I will not worship with the Hindu, nor like the Muslim go to
Mecca,
I shall serve Him and no other.
I will not pray to idols nor say the Muslim prayer.
I shall put my heart at the feet of the One Supreme Being,
For we are neither Hindus nor Mussalmans.

The death of Arjun was a turning point in the history of Punjab. He was the embodiment of many things that Nanak had preached and stood for. He had brought the Hindu and Mussalman together in creating a scripture where both were represented and in raising a temple whose foundation was laid by a Muslim and the superstructure built by Hindus and Sikhs. He was a builder of cities and a merchant-prince who brought prosperity to all communities. Arjun's blood became the seed of the Sikh church as well as of the Punjabi nation.

[This piece traced the beginnings of the Sikh faith and the teachings of the first few Gurus after Nanak. What follows is an examination of how the Sikh order changed from a peaceful one to one of militant nationalism under the tenth Guru, Gobind.—Ed]

Khushwant Singh

FROM THE PACIFIST SIKH TO
THE MILITANT KHALSA

GOBIND SINGH (1666–1708)

Gobind Rai was only nine when his father's severed head was brought to Anandpur for cremation. The shock to the child's mind and to other members of his family need not be exaggerated. The leaders of the community were concerned about the safety of Gobind, for the possibility of his being taken to Delhi as a hostage could not be ruled out. To prevent this, the young Guru and his entourage were shifted from Anandpur further into the mountains at Paonta. Gobind spent many years of his childhood in this small Himalayan town on the banks of the Yamuna. He was taught Sanskrit and Persian (in addition to the Hindi and Punjabi that he had been learning in Patna). He learned to ride and shoot, and he spent a great deal of his time hunting. The classical education and life in the mountain retreat brought out the poet in Gobind. He began to compose verses in the four languages he had learned, sometimes using all four in the same poem. He rewrote the stories of Hindu mythology in his own words, his favourite being the exploits of the Goddess Chandi, the destroyer of demons. He wrote of moonlit nights made heavy with the fragrance of wild jasmine and of lovers' trysts by the Yamuna, sparkling like a stream of quicksilver through the black mountains.

Besides schooling, hunting, and the writing of verses, there was also the serious aspect of life—Gobind's responsibilities as the leader of his community. He learned of the peaceful mission of Nanak and his four successors. He was also told of the martyrdom of Arjun and of how Arjun's son, Hargobind, had taken up arms to avenge the killing. As he grew into manhood, he was able to disentangle one strand which ran through the confusion of ideas: that although love and forgiveness are stronger than hate and revenge, once a person was convinced that the adversary meant to destroy him, it was his duty to resist the enemy with all the means at his disposal, for then it was a battle for the survival, not only of life, but of ideals. It became the dharma yudh (the battle for the sake of righteousness). His mission in life became clear to him. In his autobiography (*Apni Katha*), which forms a part of the *Bichitra Natak*, he wrote: 'I came into the world charged with the duty to uphold the right in every place, to destroy sin and evil. O ye holy men, know it well in your hearts that the only reason I took birth was to see that righteousness may flourish: that the good may live and tyrants be torn out by their roots.' In an epistle he later addressed to the Mughal emperor, he justified the method he adopted to fulfil this end. 'When all other means have failed,' he wrote in the *Zafarnama*, 'it is permissible to draw the sword'.

Gobind Rai drew the sword while he was still at Paonta. Like his grandfather, Hargobind, he let it be known that he would welcome offerings in arms and horses; and, more than the offerings, he would welcome able-bodied men willing to join his crusade. Also like his grandfather, he made sure that his crusade would not be wrongly construed as one of Sikhs against Muslims: the nucleus of his private army consisted of 500 Pathan mercenaries.

The Guru's troubles came from an unexpected quarter. He had been encouraged by the Rajput chiefs of the hills to believe that they would support him against the Mughals. But as soon as he started organizing his army, Raja Bhim Chand of Bilaspur, in whose territory Anandpur was located, turned hostile and successfully pressed the chiefs of several neighbouring hill states to try and expel the Guru from their midst. They did not like the growing power of the Guru in their region, nor, what appeared to them as an even greater danger, the increasing insubordination of the lower castes, who had begun to turn to the casteless fraternity of the Sikhs for leadership. When threats failed to dislodge the Guru, the chiefs tried to eject him by force. They bought over Gobind's Pathan mercenaries and then attacked him. Gobind Singh met their combined forces six miles out of Paonta at a place called Bhangani. Despite the desertions and numerical superiority of the Rajputs and Pathans, the Sikhs (most of whom were Hindus of the trading castes) carried the day.

The battle of Bhangani was fought in 1686. It was Gobind's first baptism in steel. The victory at Bhangani gave Gobind Rai confidence to descend from the mountains to his ancestral home in Anandpur. The attitude of the feudal overlord, Bhim Chand of Bilaspur, also changed. He was now looking for someone to organize the hill chiefs to resist the Mughal governor, who was on his way to collect arrears of revenue. Bhim Chand asked the Guru to lead the hill men against the Mughals.

The Guru's second battle was fought at Nadaun in 1687—a few months after his return to Anandpur. The initial engagement was won by the confederates led by Gobind. Despite the victory, the hill chiefs decided to come to terms with the Mughal commander and thus avoid the likelihood of another force being sent against them. Gobind refused to enter into these discussions. After spending eight days at Nadaun, he returned to Anandpur.

The Mughal Emperor Aurangzeb did not approve of the settlement which condoned a defiance of his authority, and he sent his own son Moazzam (later Bahadur Shah I) and General Mirza Beg to Punjab. The general proceeded to the hills and quickly reduced the hill chiefs to subservience. It seems that Mirza Beg had secret instructions not to bother the Guru. Gobind was left unmolested for twelve years and was able to turn his unbounded energy to reorganizing his community.

The first thing the Guru did was to fortify the centre at Anandpur. He bought the neighbouring land and built a chain of fortresses— Anandgarh, Keshgarh, Lohgarh, and Fatehgarh. Although the foothills between the Sutlej and the Yamuna where these fortresses were built lay in the territories of the Rajput chiefs, the Guru became more powerful than them.

The twelve years at Anandpur were also full of intellectual activity. Gobind selected five of the most scholarly of his disciples and sent them to Benares to learn Sanskrit and the Hindu religious texts, to be better able to interpret the writings the Gurus, which were full of allusions to Hindu mythology and philosophy. These five began the school of Sikh theologians known as the nirmalas (the unsullied).

Poets from many parts of northern India sought Gobind's

patronage and at one time fifty-two bards were in residence at the Guru's court. Since Gobind was himself a poet of considerable talent, his own preference for heroic poetry set the pattern of the compositions. Every evening the Sikhs heard ballads extolling the deeds of warriors who had defied tyranny by the force of arms. A martial atmosphere came to pervade the Sikh court at Anandpur.

In Anandpur the Guru wrote and brought up his family. Four sons, Ajit Singh, Jhujhar Singh, Zorawar Singh, and Fateh Singh, were born to his two wives, Sundari and Jito. He spent much time pondering the disunity and decadence that had come into the movement launched by Nanak. He was able to put his finger on the two causes which had contributed to this state of affairs: the wrangling over the succession to the guruship and the masands.

Belief in the spiritual tutelage of the Guru was an integral part of Nanak's teachings. Gobind felt that a living mentor could now be dispensed with, provided he could be replaced by some institution which discharged the same functions. The examples of Prithi Chand, Dhirmal, Mehrban, and Ram Rai, each of whom had disputed the succession in their time and set up as rival Gurus, were no doubt the deciding factor in Gobind's mind. Although he had four sons of his own, he felt that it would be better to end the line of personal gurus and invest the guruship in something permanent and inviolable. There was the Granth Sahib, by then well established as the book par excellence for people seeking spiritual guidance. On matters other than spiritual, there was the institution of the panchayat, with which all Punjabis were familiar. All that was needed was to adapt the panchayat to the needs of the time. Between the two, i.e., the Granth and the elected representatives of the community (panth), both the spiritual and secular functions of the Guru could be taken care of: the Granth could become the spiritual Guru, the panth itself the secular Guru, and the combination of the two, the mystic entity—the guru granth panth.

Before giving practical shape to these ideas Gobind decided to abolish the institution of masands which had become a fertile cause of disruption in the community. Many masands had set themselves up as Gurus in their own districts and had begun to nominate their own successors. Instead of propagating Sikhism and forwarding the collections they made to the Guru, many of them engaged in moneylending and trading on the 'offerings' they extorted from the poor peasants. Gobind realized that the abolition of the masands would for some time deprive the central exchequer of its only source of income. Nevertheless, he felt that the risk was worth taking and might in the end prove beneficial. He did not compromise with half measures like trying to reform the masands or separating the less corrupt from the thoroughly corrupt, but with one stroke of his pen pronounced an excommunication on the lot of them.

Gobind had to give his people something positive to replace what he had destroyed. He had created a martial atmosphere and an expectancy of military action. His father's murder was still unavenged, and the persecution of religious minorities continued as before.

Gobind had already written about his life's mission. He decided to proclaim it and take practical steps to fulfil it. Early in 1699 he sent messages inviting his followers to make a special effort to come to Anandpur for the festival of the first of Baisakh. He specifically exhorted the Sikhs to come with their hair and beards unshorn.

The crowd that collected at Anandpur is said to have been great. After the morning service the Guru appeared before the congregation, drew his sword out of its scabbard, and demanded five men for sacrifice. After some trepidation one rose to offer himself. He was taken into a tent. A little later the Guru reappeared in front of the throng with his sword dripping with blood and asked for another victim. In this manner five men were taken for a 'sacrifice' into the tent. Then the Guru came out with the five 'victims' (he had slaughtered goats instead) and announced that the Panj Piyare (five beloved ones) were to be the nucleus of a new community he would raise which was to be called the Khalsa or The Pure.

He baptized the five men in a new manner. He mixed sugar in plain water and churned it with a double-edged dagger, to the recitation of hymns, including some of his own compositions. The five who had until then belonged to different Hindu castes (one was probably a Brahmin, one a Kshatriya, and the remaining three of lesser castes) were made to drink out of one bowl to signify their initiation into the casteless fraternity or the Khalsa. Their Hindu names were changed and they were given one family name: 'Singh', for thenceforth their father was Gobind Singh (so renamed after his own baptism), their mother Sahib Devan, and their place of birth Anandpur. The baptism symbolized a rebirth, by which the initiated were considered as having renounced their previous occupations (krit nas) that of soldiering; of having severed their familial ties (kul nas) to become the family of Gobind; of having rejected their earlier creeds (dharma nas) for the creed of the Khalsa; of having given up all ritual (karm nas) save that sanctioned by the Sikh faith.

Five emblems were prescribed for the Khalsa. They were to wear their hair and beard unshorn (kesh); they were to carry a comb (kangha) in the hair to keep it tidy; they were always to wear a knee-length pair of breeches (kachha), worn by soldiers of the times; they were to carry a steel bracelet (karha) on their right wrist; and they were to be ever armed with a sabre (kirpan). In addition to these five emblems, the converts were to observe four rules of conduct (rahat): not to cut any hair on any part of their body (this was a repetition of the oath regarding the kesh); not to smoke, chew tobacco, or consume alcoholic drinks; not to eat an animal which had been slaughtered by being bled to death, as was customary with the Muslims, but only jhatka meat, where the animal had been despatched with one blow; and not to molest the person of Muslim women (this was later widened to forbid carnal knowledge of any woman other than one's wife).

At the end of the oath-taking the Guru hailed the converts with a new form of greeting:

Wahe Guruji ka Khalsa
Wahe Guruji ki Fateh

The Khalsa are the chosen of God
Victory be to our God.

Having initiated the five Sikhs, Gobind asked them to baptize him into the new fraternity. The Guru was no longer their superior; he had merged his entity in the Khalsa.

Gobind Singh is said to have explained these innovations in a lengthy address to the assemblage: 'I wish you all to embrace one creed and follow one path, obliterating all differences of religion. Let the four Hindu castes, who have different rules laid down for them in the shastras abandon them altogether and, adopting the way of cooperation, mix freely with one another. Let no one deem himself superior to another. Do not follow the old scriptures. Let none pay heed to the Ganges and other places of pilgrimage which are considered holy in the Hindu religion, or adore the Hindu deities, such as Rama, Krishna, Brahma, and Durga, but all should believe in Guru Nanak and his successors. Let men of the four castes receive baptism, eat out of the same vessel, and feel no disgust or contempt for one another.'

The news writer of the Mughal court who was present on the occasion wrote in his report that: 'When the Guru had thus addressed the crowd several Brahmins and Khatris stood up and said that they accepted the religion of Nanak and of the other Gurus. Others, on the contrary, said that they would never accept any religion which was opposed to the teaching of the Vedas and shastras, and that they would not renounce at the bidding of a boy the ancient faith which had descended to them from their ancestors. Thus, though several refused to accept the Guru's religion, about twenty thousand men stood up and promised to obey him, as they had the fullest faith in his divine mission.'

The turbulent period that followed this baptismal ceremony did not give the Guru much time to explain the significance of the symbols he made obligatory for his followers. But they are not very difficult to understand. The chief symbol was the wearing of the hair and beard unshorn. This had been customary amongst ascetics in India from time immemorial. There is reason to believe that all the Gurus after Nanak and many of their disciples had abstained from cutting their hair. (The injunction did not surprise the Sikhs, since it was not really an innovation.) By making it obligatory for his followers, Gobind intended to raise an army of soldier-saints who would wield arms only in a righteous cause, as would saints if they were so compelled. Other emblems were complementary to this one and the profession of soldiering.

A more important question than the significance of the new forms was: did Gobind mean to change the faith of Nanak? Yes and no.

In its essential beliefs Gobind introduced no change. His Sikhism was that of Nanak, believing in the One Supreme Creator who was without form or substance and beyond human comprehension. He condemned the worship of idols. He gave the institution of guruship a permanent and abiding character by vesting it in the immortality of the Granth and in the continuity of the Khalsa Panth. Being the author of so many traditions, he was particularly conscious of the danger of his followers imposing divinity on him.

> For though my thoughts were lost in prayer
> At the feet of Almighty God,
> I was ordained to establish a sect and lay down its rules.
> But whosoever regards me as Lord
> Shall be damned and destroyed.
> I am—and of this let there be no doubt—
> I am but the slave of God, as other men are,
> A beholder of the wonders of creation.
>
> (*Bichitra Natak*)

Like Nanak, Gobind Singh believed that the sovereign remedy for the ills of mankind was naam—a life of prayer. He did not alter the form of prayer—the Adi Granth remained the scripture; his own works were never accorded the same sanctity. He disapproved of asceticism and ridiculed the caste system. His motto was: maanas ki jaat sab ek hi pahchanbo—know all mankind as one caste. Like Nanak, he believed that the end of life's journey was the merging of the individual in God:

> As sparks flying out of a flame
> Fall back on the fire from which they rise,
> As dust rising from the earth
> Falls back upon the same earth;
> As waves beating upon the shingle
> Recede and in the ocean mingle
> So from God come all things under the sun
> And to God return when their race is run.
>
> (*Akal Ustat*)

The only change Gobind brought about in the religion was to expose the other side of the medal. Whereas Nanak had propagated goodness, Gobind Singh condemned evil. One preached the love of one's neighbour, the other the punishment of transgressors. Nanak's God loved His saints; Gobind's God destroyed His enemies.

It would be idle to pretend that this change of emphasis was purely theological. The results were visible within a few months of the famous baptismal ceremony, when a sect of pacifists was suddenly transformed into a militant brotherhood of crusaders. The hills around Anandpur began to echo to the beating of war drums and military commands. Gobind ordained that the day after the Hindu festival of Holi in spring was to be celebrated with mock battles between parties of Sikhs.

The complexion of the Sikh community also underwent a radical change. Up until that time the leadership had remained in the hands of the non-militant urban Khatris from whom the masands had been drawn. They had been quite willing to pay lip service to the ideal of a casteless society preached by Nanak, but they were not willing to soil their lips by drinking amrit out of the same bowl, as Gobind wanted them to do. Few of them accepted conversion to the new faith. They remained just Sikhs, better known as Sahajdharis (those who take time to adopt) and separated from the Keshadhari (hirsute) Khalsa. The bulk of the converts were Jat peasants of the central districts of Punjab who were technically low in the caste hierarchy. They took over the leadership from the Khatris. The rise of militant Sikhism became the rise of Jat power in Punjab.

Sikh chronicles maintain that the baptism of twenty thousand Sikhs at Anandpur was followed by mass baptisms all over northern India. The Guru had dinned into the timid peasantry of Punjab that they must 'take the broom of divine knowledge and sweep away the filth of timidity'. Thus did Gobind 'train the sparrow to hunt the hawk and one man to fight a legion'. Within a few months a new people were born—bearded, beturbanned, fully armed, and with a crusader's zeal to build a new commonwealth. They implicitly believed that

The Khalsa shall rule.

Their enemies will be scattered.

Only they that seek refuge will be saved.

The eruption of this large and aggressive community in their midst made the hill chiefs, particularly the Raja of Bilaspur extremely nervous. They realized that if they did not do something about it, the wrath of the Mughal government would fall on them.

The Raja of Bilaspur consulted his fellow chiefs, and they agreed that the Guru should be ejected from the hills. First they tried to provoke him. Bilaspur asked him to pay rent for the territory he occupied. Gobind replied that the lands had been bought freehold by his father and no rent was due. The hillmen encircled Anandpur and stopped supplies of food grains. The Sikhs, led by Gobind's eldest son, Ajit Singh, who was only a lad of fourteen, broke through the cordon more than once, but eventually the difficulty of getting supplies regularly could not be overcome and the Guru moved out of Anandpur to a small village called Nirmoh near Kiratpur. The Raja of Bilaspur tried to ambush his forces but was defeated and paid the price of having several of his villages plundered in retaliation.

The hill chiefs realized that the Guru was too strong for them, and they petitioned the emperor for help. Mughal forces from Sirhind and Lahore joined the hillmen and invested the Guru at Nirmoh. The Khalsa held them at bay and, after twenty-four hours of continuous fighting, broke through the besiegers. They also defeated an attempt by the Mughals to circumvent them. The Guru found refuge in Basali. The Raja of Bilaspur made one more attempt to annihilate his forces but, badly beaten, made terms with the Guru, and the Khalsa returned to Anandpur.

Gobind Singh began to prepare himself for the more serious trouble that he knew lay ahead of him. Until then Anandpur was a fortress in name only with a few turrets on the sides of a steep hill. He had it surrounded by a massive wall and stocked it with weapons of war.

The trouble he had anticipated was not long in coming. The hill rajas again approached the emperor and warned him of the growing power of the Guru. Aurangzeb ordered the subedars (district governors) of Sirhind and Lahore to help the rajas destroy the Khalsa. Anandpur was again besieged by a combination of hillmen and Mughals. The stock of food in Anandpur ran out and the attempts to break out of the town were frustrated. The Sikhs held on doggedly until the besiegers were as wearied of fighting as they. The Mughals offered Gobind safe conduct if he evacuated Anandpur. Gobind then set fire to his stores and evacuated the fort with his family and a small band of soldiers who remained with him. He had not gone very far when, contrary to their most solemn oaths, the imperial forces and the hillmen came in pursuit. Gobind entrusted his mother, wife, and two of the younger sons to a Brahmin servant and proceeded southwards. A band of Sikhs under the command of Udai Singh fell back and held the pursuers until they were killed to a man. The rearguard action gave the Guru time to reach Chamkaur, where he and forty men who were left with him built a stockade and decided to fight to the finish.

The gallant little band kept the enemy at bay. Every few hours, some of them would issue forth and fight the besiegers until they were killed. Amongst those who fell at Chamkaur were Gobind's elder sons, Ajit Singh and Jhujhar Singh. When all seemed lost, a Sikh who resembled Gobind Singh put on the Guru's clothes and, like the rest of the party, went out of the stockade to fight. While the besiegers were celebrating their kill, the Guru himself made his escape.

The Guru's life was saved by two Pathans he had known earlier. At Machiwara, where the imperial troops again closed in on him, the Pathans put Gobind in a curtained palanquin and passed the Mughal sentries with the explanation that they were carrying their pir. That was the end of the pursuit as far as the Guru was concerned. He arrived in the village of Jatpura, weary of limb but still full of faith and courage. 'I shall strike fire under the hoofs of your horses,' he wrote to Aurangzeb, 'and I will not let you drink the water of my Punjab.'

At Jatpura he learned of the execution of his two remaining sons, Zorawar Singh, aged nine, and Fateh Singh, aged seven, and the death of his own mother from shock. Gobind took the news with stoic calm. 'What use is it to put out a few sparks when you raise a mighty flame instead?' he wrote.

The news of the dastardly murders spread all over the countryside and thousands of Sikhs flocked to the Guru's camp at Kot Kapura to help him avenge the crime. At Kot Kapura, Gobind got news that Wazir Khan's forces were marching against him. The Guru now had enough men with him to make a stand. At the village of Khidrana, he turned on his pursuers and scattered them. The village was renamed Muktsar (Pool of Salvation).

The Guru spent almost a year in the country around Muktsar. The stay was most fruitful, for hundreds of thousands of Jats of the Malwa region accepted baptism and joined the Khalsa fraternity; amongst them were the ancestors of the houses of Patiala, Nabha, and Jind whose families had already become Sikhs. Gobind retired for some time to the village of Talwandi Sabo (now called Dam Dama, 'breathing place'), where he busied himself with his disciple Mani Singh, preparing a definitive edition of the Granth and collecting his own writings which were subsequently put together by Mani Singh and entitled *Dasven Padshah ka Granth* (the Granth of the Tenth Emperor) or the Dasam Granth, distinct from the first or the Adi Granth. The months of intense literary activity gave Dam Dama the new title Guru ki Kasi (Benares of the Guru).

From Dam Dama Gobind sent a letter to the emperor telling him of the perfidy of his officials, particularly of the crime committed by Wazir Khan of Sirhind. Gobind's emissary travelled to the Deccan and succeeded in handing the letter to the emperor. Aurangzeb was apparently moved by the contents of the letter and issued orders that the Guru was not to be molested any further. But Aurangzeb either did not want to or was unable to punish Wazir Khan. Gobind left Dam Dama to go and see Aurangzeb himself. He got as far as Rajputana when he heard of the death of the emperor at Ahmednagar on 2 March 1707.

The battle for succession started between Aurangzeb's sons. Bahadur Shah had shown consideration to Gobind in his troubles with the hill chiefs. Gobind felt it was his turn to help the prince and he sent a detachment of Sikh horsemen who fought in the battle of Jajau on 8 June 1707. When Bahadur Shah was firmly in the royal seat, Gobind came to Agra to pay him a formal visit. He was welcomed and given a jewelled scarf and presents worth Rs 60,000. Gobind stayed in Agra for four months, but the emperor did not take any action on behalf of the Guru against Wazir Khan, and left for Rajputana. Gobind and his retinue of horsemen accompanied the imperial troops without participating in any of their battles.

Bahadur Shah turned towards the Deccan to suppress the rebellion of his brother Kam Baksh. Gobind and his band also went south. They arrived in Nanded, a small town on the banks of the Godavari, in September 1707, and encamped there.

All along the march the Guru continued instructing his followers and those who cared to come to his prayer meetings. His guards were not allowed to question or stop anyone. One evening two young Pathans entered his tent and, finding the Guru alone, stabbed him in the abdomen. The motive for the murderous assault was never known, since the assassins were slain immediately. The Guru's wounds were stitched and it was hoped that he would recover. But the stitches burst a few days later and Gobind realized that his end was near. He assembled his followers and told them the line of Gurus was to end with him and the Sikhs were thereafter to look upon the Granth as the symbol of all the ten Gurus and their constant guide. The Guru died an hour and a half after midnight on 7 October 1708.

Gobind Singh was the beau idéal of Punjabis. He was a handsome man, whose feats as a cavalier, swordsman, and archer were enough to endear him to a people who set store by physical prowess. Stories of his prodigious strength and valour multiplied, and he became a legendary figure in his lifetime. The tips of his arrows were said to be mounted with gold to provide for the family of the foe they killed and he was reputed to be able to send his shafts as far as the eye could see. Punjabis pictured him leading them to battle on his roan stallion. On one hand fluttered his white hawk, in the other flashed his sabre. Their favourite titles for him were: the rider of the blue horse (nile ghore da asvaar), the lord of the white hawks (Chitian baajaan wala), and the wearer of plumes (kalgi-dhar). While Gobind's picture was in the minds of the people, his words were on their lips. For the amante, there was the sensuous poetry of the earlier days at Paonta; for the downcast, there was the inspiration and reaffirmation of faith; for the defeated, there was the Epistle of Victory (Zafarnama), breathing defiance in every line; for the crusader, there were the heroic ballads full of martial cadence in their staccato lines with a beat like that of a war drum. Above all, in everything he wrote or spoke or did, there was a note of buoyant hope (charhdi kala) and the conviction that even if he lost his life, his mission was bound to succeed.

The two hundred years between Nanak's proclamation of faith (1499) and Gobind's founding of the Khalsa Panth (1699) can be neatly divided into two almost equal parts. In the first hundred years, the five Gurus pronounced the ideals of a new social order for Punjab. The religion was to be one acceptable to both the Muslims and Hindus; it was to be monotheistic, non-idolatrous, and free of meaningless form and ritual. The social order was to embrace all the people; no class was to be beyond the pale, and even though the caste system continued to count when it came to making matrimonial alliances, it was abolished in matters of social intercourse. The doors of Sikh temples were thrown open to everyone and in the Guru's langar the Brahmin and the untouchable broke their bread as members of the same family. The code of this new order was the non-denominational anthology of hymns, the Granth; its symbol, the Harmandir, an edifice whose first stone was laid by a Muslim, the rest being built by Hindus and Sikhs together.

It is not surprising that the Sikhism of the first five Gurus and the Granth found ready acceptance amongst the masses. They responded to it because it was eclectic, simple, and propounded by men who were too modest either to claim kinship with God or to clothe their utterances in the garb of prophecy. What they wrote or said had a familiar ring in the people's ears. Hindus caught the wisdom of the Vedas, of which they knew but little because of the monopoly over Sanskrit learning maintained by the Brahmins. The Muslims were reminded of the exhortations of the Sufis. To both the Hindus and the Muslims, the message of the Gurus came in a language they understood. Although this fact prejudiced the spreading of Sikhism to those who could not understand Punjabi, within Punjab its appeal was irresistible. It had all the elements of a national faith and, until it crystallized into a distinct sect with a political purpose, it continued to excite the admiration of all Punjabis.

The second period of a hundred years saw the development of traditions which supplemented this social order. The sixth guru was the first to appeal to arms; the tenth put the army on a regular footing. The movement also found its martyrs and heroes: Arjun, Tegh Bahadur, and the sons of Gobind wore the crown of martyrdom; Hargobind and Gobind, the halo of heroism. The movement had its hard inner core consisting of nearly a hundred thousand baptized Khalsa, and a much larger number of close associates amongst the Sahajdhari Sikhs. The movement had the active support of the vast majority of Punjabi Hindus who joined it in large numbers and for a time gave it the semblance of Hindu resistance against the onslaught of Islam. This was particularly so in the years following the death of Guru Gobind Singh, when the Muslim ruling class exploited the religious sentiments of the Muslim masses and for a time were able to stem the rising tide of Punjabi nationalism.

WRITING SIKH HISTORY

For one who is not a trained historian, the three big problems are the paucity of original documents, the method of interpreting those that are discovered, and finally, having to decide whether or not their contents are 'history'. I will illustrate these points with my experience of four years of research in Sikh history. I have no training as a historian and some of my observations may appear naive. But as I have had to telescope learning history and writing it into one piece, I am in a position to question the material on which many histories are based and suggest reasons why histories of India tend invariably to be 'periodized' and make desperately dull reading.

The history of the Sikhs is assumed to begin with Guru Nanak who was born in 1469 and died seventy years later in 1539. He did not attain prominence till he proclaimed his faith in the year 1500. Thereafter, he spent so much of his time wandering over Asia—from Assam to Basra, from Tibet to Ceylon—that no one was able to keep pace with him. On some of his travels, he was accompanied by a Muslim minstrel called Mardana, at others by a peasant named Bala or people of whom nothing is known besides their names.

Guru Nanak made no record of his journeys and only few of his hymns refer to actual incidents. More frequently, incidents were fabricated to make a setting for his hymns. Mardana wrote nothing except a few verses which were later incorporated into the Adi Granth. Other companions of Nanak were completely illiterate. The chief source for the life of the Guru is a biography—*Janam Sakhi*—said to have been dictated by Bala. This *Janam Sakhi* has caused Sikh historians endless trouble. It is in rustic dialect and crammed with fairy tales, which the most devout shudder to accept. Fifty years ago, the late Bhai Vir Singh subjected Bala's *Janam Sakhi* to a searching analysis and proved beyond doubt that it was spurious and that we could not be even sure whether there was any such person as Bala who was a companion to the Guru.

There is little doubt that some of the miracles associated with Nanak were the stock-in-trade miracles ascribed to the Bhakti and Sufi saints of the time. The cobra shading the infant avatar with its hood, and the disappearance of the body of the Guru while his Hindu and Muslim disciples clamoured for its possession appear in the life of Kabir. The parable of returning a bowl of milk with a jasmine in it (to indicate that even if the world is full of goodness as the bowl is full of milk there is still room for fragrance in it) is ascribed to many Sufi divines. It was an age of plagiarism in which writings, incidents, miracles—everything—was freely borrowed without acknowledgement. What then are we left with in reconstructing the life of the founder-Guru? There are many other Janam Sakhis—all based on that of 'Bala' or something which closely resembled 'Bala's'.

SOURCE MATERIALS

The only authentic material historians are left with are relics at places the Guru visited (inscribed stones have been found in East Bengal, Assam and one near Basra), his own compositions and the writings of contemporary scholars relating to incidents of common experience. Thus we know that at the time of Nanak, the reigning dynasty was the Lodi and that the local zamindar of Talwandi was one Rai Bular. But we do not know whether the Guru was really imprisoned by Babur who then repented his misdeeds (as Sikh historians claim) because the *Tuzuk-i-Babari* has no reference to this meeting (perhaps Nanak was not then as famous a saint as he became later). Basically, this is all the material that a biographer can really trust; the rest is inference and conjecture.

By the time Guru Nanak died, his movement was well and properly launched. It attracted the attention of Mughal subedars and the official Waqa-i-Navis began to send in regular reports. This was more so after the execution of the fifth Guru, Arjun (1606) when the Sikhs began to transform themselves from a pacifist to a militant sect. The succeeding Gurus had their own bards who recorded important events. These two sources provide two opposite versions from which a discerning and honest historian can get a reasonably accurate picture of the period. This phenomenon, however, ends with the Gurus. After the death of Guru Gobind (1708) the historian is left with only one source, the official anti-Sikh one because the Sikhs themselves abandoned the pen for the sword.

The rise and fall of Banda (1708–16) and the struggles of the Sikh misls against Mughal subedars and Ahmed Shah Abdali who invaded Punjab nine times between 1747 and 1765 are largely based on Afghan and Mughal accounts. Non-Muslim historians usually extract compliments to the Sikhs (which are rare) and delete derogatory references; abusive epithets invariably used for the Sikhs were 'black-faced' or 'bearded dogs'. As the Sikh misldars elevated themselves from common freebooters to chieftains, they acquired their own bards and news writers. Thereafter, we get a mass of family histories—many of which were utilized by [Lepel H.] Griffin to compile his voluminous *Chiefs and Families of Note in Punjab*. With the advent of Ranjit Singh, the source material becomes enormous. Accounts by European travellers; political correspondence between the Durbar and the East India Company; Mughal, Gurkha, Rajput, Afghan and Maratha news writers' reports; and, of course, the detailed entries of court historians like Sohan Lal Suri whose *Umdat-ut-Tawarikh* even records the maharaja's bowel movements. Thereafter, the problem is not the paucity of material, but the method of treatment.

EARLY HISTORIANS

During the eighteenth and the early nineteenth centuries, Sikhs produced historians of their own. Ratan Singh Bhangu, Gyani Gyan Singh and Santokh Singh wrote detailed accounts of their co-religionists and, to compensate for the diatribes of Muslim historians, denounced everything Islamic whether Mughal or Afghan and glorified the achievements of the Khalsa. The pattern set by these men was followed by two later historians, Karam Singh and Baba Prem Singh of Hoti Mardan to whom the present generation of Sikhs owe most of their knowledge of the misls, Ranjit Singh and wars with the British. None of these writers pretended to be objective, and strictly followed the traditional pattern of reducing history to the biographies of successive rulers. Economic conditions (apart from an occasional reference to the cost of food grains), class conflicts and social phenomena rarely obtrude in their narratives.

Sikh history in the sense in which history is used in modern times has been written by half a dozen men. Professor Indubhushan Banerjee subjected Macauliffe's six tomes of the religion of the Sikhs to a critical analysis and condensed them into two extremely compact and readable volumes entitled *Evolution of the Khalsa*. He did not go to any original sources nor add to the existent knowledge on Sikhism. The same could be said of Dr Gokul Chand Narang's *Transformation of Sikhism* which is an excellent piece of interpretative history—a forensic marshalling of well-known facts to sustain a thesis on the factors which transformed the quietist followers of Nanak to the aggressive and hirsute Khalsa of Gobind. Dr N. K. Sinha of Calcutta University broke fresh—though not very fertile—ground with his study of the rise of the misls and a short biography of Ranjit Singh. (By strange oversight he ended his narrative eight years before the death of the maharaja. Did Sinha mean to immortalize the Lion of Punjab?)

SIGNIFICANT WORKS

Punjab has produced three distinguished historians of the Sikhs—all of whom have added enormously to our information on the community. Dr Sita Ram Kohli was the first to examine the records of the Khalsa Durbar, which, but for him, would have been lost forever. His biography of Ranjit Singh, unfortunately only available in Hindi and Gurmukhi, is infinitely more detailed, accurate and objective than the sketchy works of Griffin and Sinha. Dr Kohli also completed an equally detailed account of the fall of the Sikh kingdom.

Dr Hari Ram Gupta's research on the misl period has been the most exhaustive done so far on any period of Sikh history by anyone. His three volumes are based on hitherto untapped Persian material and have undoubtedly been the basis of some of the work by Dr Sinha and the team comprising the late Professor Teja Singh and Dr Ganda Singh. Dr Gupta's otherwise invaluable work becomes somewhat prosaic because of his reluctance to propound a theme or draw conclusions.

But that may well be his view of what history should be.

The most eminent and respected contemporary Sikh historian is Dr Ganda Singh of Patiala. He has written a large number of books both in English and Gurmukhi of which three are recognized as classics—*Banda Singh Bahadur, Ahmed Shah Durrani* and an account of the Kuka movement. In all of them, battles and dynasties assume great importance. Dr Ganda Singh's dates are usually in triplicate—Vikrami, Hijri and the Christian era—along with the precise quarters of the moon.

NO THEMATIC CONTENT

Following the style current in academic circles of Punjab, all the three historians make a deliberate effort to make their histories many-sided by inserting separate chapters under such headings as 'Judicial system', 'Revenue system', 'Army', etc. Little or no attempt is made to knit these into one story or pull out the one string on which events are strung as beads on a rosary. No one, for instance, has yet propounded the most obvious theme that the rise of Sikhism was the rise of Punjabi consciousness, culminating in the formation of a Punjabi state. The absence of the thematic approach is chiefly responsible for this strange fact that these historians write finis to Sikh history on the annexation of Punjab in 1849. Captain Joseph Darey Cunningham's history of the Sikhs brings the account up to the end of the First Anglo-Sikh War in 1845.

It is a strange phenomenon that no historian has thought it fit to complete the story by writing of the last 150 years. Undoubtedly, what has daunted them is the fact that since they look upon the kingdom of Ranjit Singh as a Sikh kingdom, its fall is considered as the end of Sikh history. This is far from the truth as not only did more than half the Sikhs (the Malwais of the Cis-Sutlej region) have nothing to do with the Sikh kingdom but the so-called Sikh kingdom itself was so thoroughly Punjabi, with Muslim and Hindu ministers and generals, that labelling it 'Sikh' is almost a libel on Ranjit Singh's secularism.

THE ABSORPTION

After the end of the 'Sikh' kingdom, the history of the Sikhs is so completely mingled with that of the other communities that it becomes as difficult to separate it as it would be to separate one strand from a hank of hair. But, the thread has a distinct historical role and personality. Just as from its inception Sikhism was an expression of militant Hinduism as well as Punjabi nationalism, so too, after its nationalist role had been played, its history became one of resistance to the absorptive tendencies of resurgent Hinduism and to find a raison d'etre for its separate existence.

During my research, I came across an incident in the Second Anglo-Sikh War (1848–1849) which caused me some amusement as well as gave me food for thought. In the spring of 1849 Diwan Mulraj, the Governor of Multan, had resigned his post. Kahan Singh Man was nominated by the English Resident to replace him. Two English officers, Vans Agnew and Lieutenant Anderson, along with troops of the Durbar infantry and cavalry, had been sent with Kahan Singh to take possession of the fort. After the ceremonial handing over of the place, when the Durbar party was returning to its encampment, a mutinous soldier, angered by the order to salute the ferringees, lunged at Vans Agnew with his spear and wounded him. The disbanded Multani soldiery rallied round Vans Agnew's assailant and later in the afternoon looted the Durbar camp and carried off all provisions.

Mulraj, who was forced to become the leader of the rebellion, was presented with part of the loot. It consisted of bottles of whisky, brandy and beer. There were also hermetically sealed lead boxes. The stores were spread out in front of the Diwan for the benefit of the courtiers. The bottles were uncorked and passed round for scrutiny. The courtiers sniffed at the contents and passed the brandy and Scotch as fit for human consumption. Beer did not have a familiar smell; its pale yellow colour made it particularly suspect and it was poured out into the gutter as maila pani. The hermetically sealed boxes were the subject of much debate. The majority were of the opinion that it was a new kind of shrapnel and the best thing to do was to use it against the enemy. Next morning, Mulraj's guns opened up against the Durbar English encampment, which was without food, and pelted it with bully beef, shrimps, sardines, lobsters and other delicacies!

THE DRY APPROACH

Did this incident qualify for inclusion in a book of history? Many scholars had undoubtedly examined the records before me but no one had made use of it because they considered it too trivial. Some had extracted what they considered material of 'historic' importance, e.g., Mulraj's court was familiar with hard liquor but not beer; that by the middle of the nineteenth century the English knew how to make airtight boxes; that tin had not yet been introduced as a container and lead was used despite the danger of lead-poisoning—and so on. This sort of dry academic approach is the chief reason why our histories make such dull reading.

The British conquest of Sindh is epitomized in the one-word message sent by Napier to the Governor General: 'Peccavi (I have sinned)'. The message may have been apocryphal; but it is the stuff which sugarcoats history and makes it fascinating.

NAMDHARIS OR KUKAS

The Kuka or Namdhari movement was, like the Nirankari, a movement of religious revival. It started in the last few years of Sikh rule. The initiator, Bhagat Jawahar Mal, also known as Sain Sahib (d. 1862), and his disciple Baba Balak Singh, had a considerable reputation as men of learning and piety and attracted many followers to their centre at Hazro (North West Frontier Province) known as the Jagiasi Abhiasi Ashram.

Bhagat Jawahar Mal and Balak Singh had for their mission two objects: first, that of purging the Sikhs of some obnoxious Hindu practices which had gained currency despite the injunction of the Gurus against them, e.g., caste distinctions and taboos, incarceration of widows, and the worship of idols, tombs and ascetics; and second, that of reforming the Sikh nobility. The Sikh aristocracy, which had risen from the ranks of common peasants, had acquired enormous wealth and power. Many of these newly rich had taken to a dissolute life, of drink and debauchery. Bhagat Jawahar Mal aimed at bringing them back to the path of righteousness. The objects of the Namdhari movement were very similar to those of the Nirankari, but whereas the Nirankaris restricted their activities to religious affairs, the Namdharis got involved in political matters.

After the annexation of Punjab, the movement underwent a change. To the zeal for religious and social reformation was added a feeling of resentment against the new rulers and an ambition to restore Sikh sovereignty. The leadership of the Namdharis fell into the hands of a remarkable man who shared these feelings and was willing to risk giving them a trial. This was Ram Singh of village Bhayani in District Ludhiana.

Ram Singh (1815–1885) was the son of a carpenter. In his early youth he joined Prince Naonihal Singh's army as a soldier and served in it for eight years. Army manoeuvres took him north and he came into contact with Balak Singh. After the First Sikh War he resigned his commission and retired to his village in Bhayani, where he set himself up as a manufacturer of coats of mail. To this he added preaching and propagating the teachings of Bhagat Jawahar Mal and Balak Singh. Within a few years Ram Singh acquired a large following. On the Hindu New Year's day in 1857 he, following the precedent of Guru Gobind Singh, baptized five of his disciples as members of the new community, which he named the Namdharis. They also came to be known as Kukas because of the cries (kooks) they emitted in a state of religious frenzy. In addition to the vows prescribed by Guru Gobind, Ram Singh enjoined his Sikhs to observe other rules, which he divided into personal, social, religious and political. They were:

(a) Personal: Not to eat meat or drink alcohol.
Not to covet another's property or women.
Not to lie.
Not to accept interest on loans.

(b) Social: Not to kill female children or sell them.
Not to allow marriages of infants under the age of sixteen or arrange marriages by exchange.
Not to give expensive gifts or weddings.
Not to castrate domestic animals.

(c) Religious: To rise at dawn, bathe and pray with rosaries made with wool.
To wear their turbans straight (unlike those of other Sikhs, the two sides of whose turbans meet at an angle on the forehead).
To protect cows and other animals from slaughter.

(d) Political: Not to accept service with the government.
Not to send children to government schools.
Not to use courts of law but settle disputes in panchayats.
Not to use foreign goods. Not to use the government postal service.

All these vows were incorporated in an epistle (*Rahatnama*) which Ram Singh issued to his followers in 1863.

Within a couple of years the number of Ram Singh's followers increased to over 50,000, spread all over Punjab. He set up subas (governors) and naib subas (deputy governors) to organize the Kukas and arranged military training for them. He started his own postal service. He sent a delegation to Nepal and his gesture of friendship was reciprocated by the Nepalese court by a return of presents. Ram Singh abandoned the earlier quietist way of life. He came to be surrounded by a following of horsemen and himself rode a favourite mare and was addressed as 'Chiniwala Padshah'—'Lord of the Chini horse' (from the name of the animal).

When the English established themselves as rulers of Punjab, the only organized body of men that constantly drew their attention were the Namdharis. For some years they just watched them without undue interference. This attitude came to an end with the Mutiny. Then all native organizations became suspect. At first the government examined the Namdhari headquarters at Hazro. In 1863 a police post was set up at Bhayani and Ram Singh and his subas interned within the village limits. These restrictions were relaxed three years later, but the police continued to keep a close watch on Kuka activities for many more years.

Our evening prayers always concluded with a short invocation to the Great Guru: 'Grant us the gift of thy holy name. Grant us ablution in the sacred pool of Amritsar.'

It was not the Great Guru who granted me the gift of his holy name but my grandmother who would not give me supper till I had said my prayers. And in his divine wisdom the Great Guru did not let me visit Amritsar till I was sixteen years old. Meanwhile my expectations were heightened by tales told by those who had been to the holy city. They said that lepers who bathed in the pool were cleansed of their loathsome disease; crows that dipped into it turned white; some even claimed to have seen the silver-white falcon of the last of our ten Gurus (who had been murdered over 250 years ago) alight on the pinnacle of the temple dome and then disappear into the blue heavens. They brought back bottles full of water from the sacred pool; we received a few drops in the palms of our hands joined together, gulped them down, and then reverently smeared our eyes and foreheads with our damp hands. They brought a few morsels of dried chapattis and dal from the temple kitchen, which we ate as if it were manna. Some brought bracelets made of steel, combs made of ivory and small daggers—all emblems of the Sikh faith—and gave them to their favourite children.

Though only a little over 400 years old, Amritsar is to us Sikhs the mother of all cities. What Jerusalem is to the Jews, Rome to the Catholics and Mecca to the Muslims, Amritsar is to the Sikhs: it is their most important place of pilgrimage, the scene of many of the most important events in the 500 years of their troubled history, and the seat of authority from which religious and political encyclicals are issued.

I was in the first year at university when I first went to Amritsar. I cannot now recall whether it was what I had imagined it to be as a child. But the visit remains indelibly imprinted on the tablet of my memory. I was escorting my mother, who wished to have prayers said for the soul of her father who had died a few weeks earlier. We emerged from the crowded railway station in the early hours of a winter morning. Those days there were no taxis in Amritsar; only pony-drawn two-wheeled tongas. There was a scuffle between tonga drivers till the victor herded us and the porters carrying our baggage to his vehicle. Before I could bargain with the driver, the tonga was on the move. 'Where to?' the tonga wallah demanded.

'Darbar Sahib—the court of the holy one. How—'

'That'll be four rupees,' he snapped, lashing his skinny horse on the flanks. 'Come on, son, like the wind.'

The pony broke into a gentle trot. We found ourselves going through narrow, serpentine bazaars with balconies almost touching each other above our heads. There was barely enough room for our tonga. We had to contend with other tongas, motor cars, pedestrians, cyclists and herds of cows and buffaloes. The driver perched himself on the beam of the tonga and stuck the wooden end of his whip into the spokes of the wheel to produce a rattle. His voice did the rest: 'Look out, babuji... Sister! Sister! See where you are going! Oi, you blind one, does the angel of death hover over you?' To the buffaloes: 'Durreh, durreh, may a snake bite you!' And then again to his pony: 'Shabash, son. Like the wind.'

The tortuous ride ended at a confluence of bazaars facing a clock tower. By the time I had paid off the tonga wallah we were surrounded by beggars and coolies. A blind woman held her bowl under my mother's chin: 'May the Guru grant you seven sons!' A leper dug his stump into my ribs: 'May the Guru grant all your wishes. May your pen write cheques of lakhs of rupees.'

The coolies who had grabbed our luggage pushed their way through the throng of beggars with us following on their heels. They dumped our trunks and bedding rolls outside an enclosure. We checked in our luggage with our shoes. My mother brought a leaf-cup full of rose petals and marigolds. We washed our feet in a cistern full of dirty, muddy water and gingerly walked over slippery marble slabs towards the entrance. Suddenly the temple burst into view. A few feet below us was a large, squarish pool of water; in the middle of this pool was an edifice of white marble topped with a large golden dome and minarets. It looked as if on a plate of lapis lazuli someone had placed a jewel box made of pearls, topped with nuggets of burnished gold. I gaped at it spellbound. My mother shut her eyes and mumbled her prayers. She went down on her knees and made obeisance, rubbing her forehead on the cold marble. When she rose, her eyes were brimming with tears.

We went down the marble steps and alongside the pool. There were several small shrines marking the site of some martyrdom or other event in the history of the temple. My mother made obeisance at each one and sprinkled a few rose petals. We came to another gate leading to the marble causeway which ran through the pool. At every threshold my mother ran her palms over the floor to take the dust of pilgrims' feet and put it across her forehead. And so we made our way to the sanctum sanctorum. It was packed with worshippers. In the centre under a gold canopy was the sacred scripture, the Granth Sahib; on one side a party of hymn singers singing to the accompaniment of harmoniums and tabla drums. Men and women sat facing each other separated by a passage through which a never-ending stream of worshippers came to make their obeisance and offerings of money and flowers before the sacred book. We could find no place to sit and allowed ourselves to be pushed along. We went up a short flight of stairs; on either side, the marble was festooned with floral designs embedded with semi-precious stones like carnelian and serpentine. The roof was studded with mirrors and the walls had frescoes depicting the lives of our Gurus. At the rear of the inner shrine a few steps led into the pool: this was the Har ki Pauri (Steps of the Lord). Like other pilgrims, my mother filled her palms with the water, drank deep draughts and splashed it on her face. She filled the two bottles she had brought with her to take home. We retraced our steps over the marble causeway to circumambulate the pool. All along were men taking their ritual dip, their long hair knotted in buns and beards dripping with water. My mother went into the women's enclosure while I sat at a distance watching the grey shadows of the monstrous-sized carp in the pool. I saw my mother descend fully clothed into the icy cold water, hold her nostrils between her fingers and immerse herself. Once, twice, seven times—once each for her five children, once for her husband and lastly for herself. A few minutes later she came out radiant with a pink glow on her face, loudly chanting:

> In Ram Das's sacred pool
> have I bathed
> All my sins have been
> washed away

Ram Das (1534–81), the fourth of the ten Gurus, acquired land in 1577 CE to build a new town. He started by excavating a tank and filling it with water from a canal that ran nearby. The place came to be known as Ram Daspura after him. Ram Das was succeeded by his son, Arjun, as the fifth guru. Arjun (1563–1606) invited merchants and tradesmen to settle at Ram Daspura. He built a temple in the middle of the tank and, having compiled the Granth, installed it in the temple. Thereafter Ram Daspura came to be known as Amritsar, the 'pool of immortality', and the temple as Darbar Sahib.

Amritsar, despite being the Mecca of the Sikhs, had few Sikh inhabitants. When the British annexed their kingdom in 1849 the Sikhs formed no more than 10 per cent of the population of the city; the rest were Hindus and Muslims in somewhat equal proportion. It was only in the bloody riots and arson at the time of the partition of the country into India and Pakistan in 1947 that the Muslims of the city were driven out to Pakistan to make way for Hindu and Sikh refugees streaming into India in their hundreds of thousands. Many bazaars had been burnt down. This proved to be a blessing in disguise: the roads were widened, the area surrounding the Golden Temple including the clock tower was levelled to provide space for an archive, a museum-cum-picture gallery and reception room for visitors. Since Sikhs now came to form almost half the population of the city, the traffic to the temple increased manifold. Besides, Amritsar also became a frontier town, the Pakistan border being only thirty-two kilometres to the northwest. Its small cantonment became one of the biggest and most important in the country. A substantial proportion of the Indian Army continues to be Sikh. Amritsar in fact became three cities in one: the old city around the Golden Temple contained within the remains of battlements of ancient Sikh times; adjoining it a garden city known as the civil lines comprising spacious bungalows for civilian officers, well-to-do businessmen, doctors and lawyers; and the cantonment.

◆

On a more recent visit I went to Amritsar by air. An hour after we took off from New Delhi, the 'fasten seat belts' sign lit up on the panel above the front seat and the captain's voice came over the public address system to inform us that he was going to fly over the city and give us a bird's-eye view of the Golden Temple before landing.

The vast, flat khaki plain that had stretched endlessly from Delhi was suddenly turned into lush emerald green paddy fields and blocks of sugarcane. There were several tanks of water linked to each other by a network of water-channels. Villages were dotted about everywhere. And suddenly we were flying over a densely packed mass of mud and brick, a veritable anthill of humanity. In the centre of this crazy huddle of houses and bazaars was the huge squarish pool of deep blue water and in its middle glittered the Golden Temple. The plane did not fly directly overhead—that would be disrespectful to Sikh sentiment—but circled round at an angle giving us an excellent view.

I had been invited to speak at the convocation of the newly set-up Guru Nanak University, named after the founder of Sikhism, Nanak. I spent the morning going round the campus, which is ten kilometres from the centre of the city. Thereafter I went to Khalsa College which is close by. Then, like any Sikh would, I drove up to the Golden Temple.

Prakash Singh, the public relations officer of the temple, was an old friend. Apart from conducting parties of tourists and handing out literature on Sikhism, he edited a Gurmukhi monthly dedicated to the exposition of Sikh history and religion. He was a somewhat unusual Sikh—young, erudite, sophisticated and yet devoutly religious. I entered unannounced and found him surrounded by a motley collection of European boys and girls, all very bronzed, and grubby in their leather jerkins and shorts. Most of the boys sported blond beards, and hair which could have done with some trimming. And all of them could have done with a good scrubbing in the sacred pool. Prakash Singh leapt up from his chair, made a gesture of touching my feet, then embraced me warmly. He introduced me to his 'Dutch and German friends' and then dismissed them. 'Remember to wash your feet before you go in; have your heads covered and on no account carry any tobacco. And when you've been around, come back to my office and I'll take you to the Guru's kitchen for lunch. We feed several thousand pilgrims every day. It's quite a sight.' The boys and girls murmured words of thanks and obediently filed out of the room.

'Well,' he said, patting his beard, 'what brings you to Amritsar?'

'Spouting Sikhism to students who know more about it than I. I don't envy your job instructing foreigners who probably don't know the difference between a Sikh and a Sheikh.'

'Well,' he said pensively, 'there are many ways of looking at things. Without having to go abroad I meet people from all over the world. That can be fun. But I do get bored answering silly questions: practically everyone wants to know if the colour of the turban means anything and why all Sikhs are called Singhs. I give them the answers before they put the questions—"No, sir, the colour of the turban means nothing. Our tenth and last guru, Guru Gobind Singh (1660–1708), converted the pacifist Sikhs into a militant brotherhood he called the Khalsa, or the pure. He made us swear never to cut our hair or beards and gave us all one surname—Singh—which means lion. But though all Khalsa Sikhs are Singhs, all Singhs are not Khalsa Sikhs. Lots of Hindus bear the same name." You must have had to answer such questions when you are abroad.'

'Most of the time girls want to know whether I sleep in my turban.'

'What do you say?'

'I invite them to come and find out for themselves.'

He roared with laughter. 'If I said anything like that, they'd fire me.'

Prakash Singh insisted that I visit the new picture gallery. 'I'll introduce you to Kirpal Singh, our artist. He has painted most of them. He will take you around.'

I followed him up the stairs of the picture gallery. The three rooms in which paintings and relics of the Sikh period were on display were jammed with peasants. Prakash Singh asked one of the keepers to fetch Kirpal Singh from his studio. Sikhs do not have a great reputation in the realm of arts ('The only culture they have is agriculture,' said a Sikh-baiter once). I was curious to meet the man through whose brush the vision of the past was recreated for a whole generation of Sikhs. Would he be a frail man with long, tapering fingers?

Kirpal Singh was a world away from my concept of a painter. Although he was a handsome man with a raven black beard and sparkling eyes, there was nothing artistically frail about him. His dress was eccentric. He sported a spotless white turban. The rest of his person was draped in funereal black. 'I have renounced the world,' he explained, somewhat naively. 'I will dedicate the rest of my life to telling the saga of Sikh heroism through my pictures. Some people wear saffron to indicate renunciation. I wear black because black is more symbolic of death...death in life.' It was the sort of irony Indians are fond of indulging in. Even more inexplicable was a massive axe which he carried in his hand. Its silver blade gleamed through the folds of his black gown. 'Oh that!' he said, baring a row of white teeth, 'I just like having it with me.'

We turned to view the paintings. An attendant made way for us through the throng. The first was a large portrait of the founder of the Sikh faith. He was portrayed as a man of sixty in a cotton skullcap, a flowing white beard and a mendicant's garb. He held a begging bowl in one hand (he was against beggary and exhorted men to work) and a rosary in the other. Above the frame was the legend 'Guru Nanak Devji 1469–1539'. Beneath the picture was an English translation of the opening lines of his morning prayer:

There is one God
He is the supreme truth.
He, the creator,
Is without fear and without hate,
He, the omnipresent,
Pervades the universe.
He is not born,

Nor does He die to be born again.
By His grace shalt thou worship
Him.

Nanak's portrait attracted the largest crowd. Peasants touched the base of the frame and ran their palms across their foreheads. They shut their eyes and exclaimed loudly, 'Dhan Baba Nanak! (Saviour of the world).'
There were other paintings of Nanak's life. Amongst the many incidents of his life portrayed by Kirpal Singh, I recognized two. One showed a crowd of people standing waist-deep in water offering water to the rising sun. Nanak was shown facing the opposite direction and throwing water into the air. This incident took place at Haridwar on the Ganga. Nanak wanted to demonstrate the absurdity of offering water to the dead in heaven. When the pilgrims had asked him why he was facing the opposite direction he had replied, 'I'm watering my fields in my village. Surely if you can send water to heaven, which is more than a million miles away, I can send it to my village that is only a few hundred miles from here.' The other picture showed a Muslim remonstrating with Nanak who was shown lying on the floor. On his way to Mecca Nanak had rested with his feet pointing towards the holy Kaaba. When a Muslim accused him of showing disrespect towards Islam, Nanak had replied, 'Brother, you turn my feet in some other direction where God does not dwell.' The series on Nanak's life ended with a painting of his cremation. On the funeral pyre, instead of a corpse was a heap of flowers. On either side of the pyre were ranged his disciples—one side distinguishably Hindu by their dhotis and caste marks, the other equally identifiable by their fez caps and baggy trousers to be Muslims. They had contended for Nanak's body. The Hindus wanted to cremate him because they said he was a Hindu, the Muslims to bury him because they believed he was of their faith. It is said that Nanak's body mysteriously disappeared and flowers were found in its place, which the two groups divided between them.
Prakash Singh joined us for a while. We stood at the entrance of the Golden Temple and watched pilgrims come and go. 'The Sikh is as firm in his faith as he ever was!' exclaimed Prakash Singh. He was referring to a prophecy I had recklessly made in a history of the

Sikhs I had published in 1959 that if the Sikhs continued to give up wearing their long hair and beard at the rate they were doing, by the turn of the century they would relapse into Hinduism. I had written (and still hold on to the view) that the only real dividing line between the Sikhs and the Hindus is the Sikhs' unshorn hair and beard; that there is no such thing as a clean-shaven Sikh, he is a Hindu believing in Sikhism. I had often quoted Dr Lorimer's remark that a Sikh is only a kind of vicious Hindu.

'But you do agree that whatever the Sikhs have achieved has been achieved by them as the bearded and hirsute Khalsa—their militancy and their conquests, their spirit of enterprise. The way they dominate life in India, it is hard to believe that they form under 2 per cent of the population of the country—a third of the defence services, half of any Indian athletic team, why, three of the four Indians who got to the top of the peak?'

'It would have been more appropriate if it had the name of Guru Gobind Singh on it.'

'Sure!' he laughed, 'but you know what Sikhs are! Have you heard any good Sikh jokes lately?' He put his arm round my shoulder. 'Have you heard of the Sikh minister of irrigation and power? Well, he was being shown round a hydroelectric power station. The engineer explained how electricity was produced by the turbines and then the water used for irrigation. "No wonder our agricultural output is so poor," remarked the honourable minister, "what good is the water after power has been extracted from it!"'

Prakash Singh laughed heartily at his own joke and slapped me on the back many times. 'But seriously,' he suddenly became grave, 'you've got this business of Sikhs dying out or relapsing into Hinduism all wrong.'

◆

There is more to Amritsar than the Golden Temple. The Hindus have built a replica known as the Durgiana Mandir (Temple of the Goddess Durga). There are historic havelis of the Sikh aristocracy of olden times, beautifully laid out gardens and a couple of forts. But its narrow bazaars remain the chief attraction. I was loitering about them when I found myself at the entrance of Jallianwala Bagh. Next to the Golden Temple, it is the most popular place of pilgrimage. Indians of all races and religions come here to pay homage to the 400 men and women who were killed on 13 April 1919 when General Dyer ordered his Gurkha troops to open fire on a crowd gathered in contravention of an order forbidding the assemblage of more than five persons. The massacre at Amritsar proved to be the turning point in the history of India's freedom movement. A group of die-hards acclaimed Dyer as the defender of the empire and presented him with a sword of honour. And although he was cashiered and severely criticized by many Englishmen including Winston Churchill, Indians never forgave the British for the foul deed. Thereafter moderate Indian nationalists who stood for cooperation with their English rulers were displaced by Gandhi who denounced British rule as satanic and demanded complete independence for India.

Jallianwala is not much of a bagh (garden). It is a squarish plot of land enclosed between the high walls of houses. At its centre is a well in which many people drowned while trying to flee from the hail of Dyer's bullets. Beside it is a platform and a red column designed like a flame to symbolize the torch of liberty. A marble plaque bears the names of the martyrs. Every evening there is a son et lumière programme narrating the sequence of events which led to the massacre.

◆

The people of Amritsar speak a dialect of their own and have lots of stories bearing on their character. An Amritsari does not greet another with 'Sat Sri Akal (God is truth)' as other Sikhs do but says, 'I fall at your feet'. At times he makes a gesture by touching the other's knee. They are always inviting each other for a meal without specifying the date or the time. Such an offer of hospitality is referred to as an 'Amritsari invitation'.

It was such an invitation from an old friend, Dilbir Singh, a prosperous industrialist and prominent figure in society that took me to Amritsar during my latest visit. Dilbir Singh dresses in the smartest of Savile Row Suits and keeps a stock of premium brand Scotch. His wife wears Punjabi salwar-kameez but his daughter wears jeans and his son indulges in rock and roll. Nevertheless they are orthodox Sikhs. He greets me with an embrace loudly chanting 'Wahe Guru Ji Ka Khalsa (The Sikhs are the chosen of God)'; I reply 'Wahe Guruji ki Fateh (And victory to our God)'. After exchanging pleasantries with other members of his family we sit down to watch a programme beamed to India by Pakistani television in Lahore. 'Chivas Regal or Johnnie Walker Black Label?' Dilbir Singh asks me, opening his well-stocked drink cabinet. 'Any Scotch will do, I can't tell the difference,' I plead. 'I'll give you Something Special; it is smoother than any other Scotch.'

Pakistani television has a special programme meant for the Sikhs they drove out almost to a man not very long ago. It is designed to win the Sikhs over to their side in the event of future confrontation with India. It consists of singing of Sikh hymns recorded at the Golden Temple and highlighting the Indian government's discrimination against the Sikhs. It cuts no ice—but Sikhs enjoy being flattered by their erstwhile enemies.

'Why don't you shift your business to a safer place than Amritsar?' I asked Dilbir Singh. 'There will be more confrontations with Pakistan. One well-aimed bomb and this city will go up in flames.'

'Leave Amritsar?' he shouted back, excitedly. 'Never! I was born here; I will die here. If Amritsar dies, all the Sikhs will die with it.'

THE HARMANDIR SAHIB

If there is one place of worship in the world which welcomes people of all faiths and enshrines within it a scripture containing hymns composed by Hindus and Muslims of all castes and worships it as God incarnate, it is the Harmandir of Amritsar. Jews deny Gentiles access to their Wailing Wall, Zoroastrians forbid non-Zoroastrians entrance to their Agiaries, Catholics forbid non-Catholics from approaching their sacred relics, Hindus bar the gates of their temples to Muslims and Christians (and till recently to people of low-castes as well). Muslims deny non-Muslims admission to Mecca and Medina. Only the doors of the Harmandir, popularly known as the Darbar Sahib and the Golden Temple, are open to everyone, no matter what race or religion he or she belongs to. Everyone can participate in the worship that goes on almost round the clock and everyone can get a free meal at the Guru ka langar—the Guru's kitchen.

Just as Sikhism is itself an edifice built of Hindu bricks and Muslim mortar, so also the Sikhs' holiest shrine bears witness to its Hindu–Muslim genealogy. The third of the Sikh's ten Gurus, Guru Amar Das, received the site of the land as a gift from Emperor Akbar on the occasion of his daughter's wedding. Guru Amar Das's son-in-law, Ram Das, who had represented the Guru in the Mughal court had a tank dug on the site. When he succeeded his father-in-law as the fourth Guru of the Sikhs, he decided to build a new town around the tank. *The Amritsar Gazeteer* of 1883–84 records that 'in the year 1577 he [Guru Ram Das] obtained a grant of the site, together with 500 bighas of land, from the Emperor Akbar, on payment of Rs 700 to the Zamindar of Tung, who owned the land'. Guru Ram Das shifted the headquarters of the Sikh faith from Goindwal to the new township which came to be known after him as Guru Ka Chak, Chak Ram Das or Ram Das

Pura. He invited traders to set up their businesses in the town.

Guru Ram Das had three sons, of whom he considered the youngest, Arjun Mal, to be the most suited to succeed him. When Ram Das died in 1581, Arjun became the fifth Guru of the Sikhs. It was he who raised the Harmandir in the midst of the tank. In keeping with the eclectic spirit of Sikhism, he invited a Muslim divine, Hazrat Mian Meer of Lahore, to lay the foundation stone of the temple.

Two aspects of the architecture of the Harmandir deserve notice. Instead of building the shrine on a high plinth as was the Hindu custom, Arjun had it built on a lower level than the surrounding land so that worshippers would have to go down the steps to enter it. When it was represented to Arjun that the temple should be the highest building in the locality, he is reported to have replied: 'No, what is humble shall be exalted. The more a tree is laden with fruit, the more its branches descend to the earth. By whatever way you approach the temple, you must descend eight to ten steps, therefore let the Harmandir be the lowest edifice of all.' The second feature was that whereas Hindu temples had only one entrance, the Harmandir had four—representing the four Hindu castes—Brahmin, Kshatriya, Vaishya and Shudra. All were welcome.

After the temple was completed and the tank filled with water, it was given a new name, Amrit (nectar) Sar (tank) or the pool of immortality. The city itself came to be known as the 'House of Praise', Amritsar, siftee da ghar. Guru Arjun composed a special hymn on the occasion: 'Santaan ke kaaraj aap khaloya': God himself came and did the work of saints; into the beautiful land and the beautiful tank he poured nectar... bathing in the tank is equal to bathing in the 68 places of pilgrimage, to the bestowal of alms; and the performance of great purifications.' A couplet which is on the lips of pilgrims who visit Amritsar runs:

Ram Das Sarovar naahtey
Utrey sab paap kamaatey

He who bathes in the tank of Ram Das
Is washed of all sins committed by him.

A few years after the building of the Harmandir, Guru Arjun retired to a neighbouring wood where under the bosky shade of peepal, fig and neem trees he set about compiling an anthology of sacred hymns. He welcomed contributions from different sects of Hindus and Muslims. The tank was completed in the year 1604 and the Adi Granth, as it came to be known, was formally installed in the Harmandir with a senior disciple, Baba Buddha, as the first reader or granthi.

Mischief-makers did not take long to fill the ears of Emperor Akbar with false reports that the Adi Granth contained passages vilifying Islam. On his way north from Agra, Akbar stopped near Amritsar and asked Guru Arjun to let him examine the book. Bhai Buddha and another disciple, Bhai Gurdas, called on the emperor and asked him to open the volume anywhere he liked. By a strange coincidence, the page opened by Akbar had Guru Arjun's own compilation in Persian:

> From earth to light God made the world.
> The sky, earth, trees and water are God's creation.
> Man, whatever your eye perceives is perishable.

The second hymn that Emperor Akbar examined was:

> You tied a stone to your neck,
> And saw not God who dwells in your heart.
> O infidel, you wandered astray in error.
> You churned water and shall die in agony.
> The stone which you callest God
> Shall take you with it and drown you.
> O Sinner, untrue to your salt,
> It is not a boat of stone which will ferry you over.
> On meeting the guru, Nanak recognized the Lord.

◆

The Harmandir was razed to the ground by the Afghan conqueror Ahmed Shah Abdali many times and had to be rebuilt. It was finally built in its present shape in marble and gold leaf by Maharaja Ranjit Singh (whose wife Mehtab Kaur built the Shrine of the Sufi, Data Ganj Bakhsh in Lahore). An inscription above the entrance of the central shrine reads:

The Great Guru in His wisdom looked upon Maharaja Ranjit Singh as his chief servitor and Sikh, and in his benevolence, bestowed on him the privilege of serving the temple.

Periodically, water is drained out of the pool of immortality and a massive cleansing operation (kaar seva) is undertaken to remove the silt accumulated over the years. Just about everyone, be he Sikh, Hindu or Muslim is welcome to partake in the service. When it was first undertaken in 1922, hundreds of thousands of volunteers who participated swore that they saw the white hawk of Guru Gobind Singh flash down from the blue heavens and alight on the golden pinnacle of the dome. Such was the religious fervour that the temple aroused amongst its worshippers.

The birthdays of the Sikh Gurus and anniversaries of the martyrdom of Guru Arjun and the ninth Guru, Tegh Bahadur, are celebrated with great enthusiasm in the Harmandir. The most elaborate of all celebrations, however, is of the Hindu festival of Diwali. (Sikhs celebrate all Hindu festivals.) Sikh association with Islam was kept alive till 1947 by the selection of the principal party of hymn singers from a Muslim family. Until recently, almost a quarter of all pilgrims coming to the Harmandir were Hindus. A majority of Hindus of Western Punjab did in fact treat the Adi Granth as their religious scripture because they could understand its language whereas they couldn't understand the Vedas or Upanishads.

What the Harmandir means to devotees can best be witnessed near the main entrance of the temple. Parties of pilgrims approach, merrily chatting and quarrelling amongst themselves. Suddenly, the golden dome of the temple, rising above the sparkling blue waters of the surrounding pool, hoves into view. They fall silent as if spellbound. Palms are joined in prayer; some are overcome with emotion and tears flow down their cheeks. They prostrate themselves on the ground and murmur their thanks.

The best time to visit the temple is the early hours of the morning (amrit-vela—the ambrosial hour) as kirtan begins in the sanctum sanctorum—when the night washed by dew and stars gives way to the dawn. It is then that the message of Guru Arjun comes through:

Na koee bairee na begaana
Sagal sung hamree ban aiee

We have no enemies, for us there are no strangers.
Towards one and all we have goodwill.

THE ORIGINS OF PUNJABI
LANGUAGE AND LITERATURE

LANGUAGE

There are conflicting views on the origin of the Punjabi language. We are not sure what language the people of the region spoke before the Aryan invasions. Whatever it was, it soon came under the linguistic domination of Sanskrit. Thereafter the Sanskrit of the Aryans mingled with the languages spoken by the Jat tribes which had migrated from Rajasthan into Punjab. The melange produced a variety of regional dialects like Hindko, Multani, Pothohari, Majhi, Malwai, Puadhi, Doabi, Dogri and Pahari. Punjabi of the eleventh century was then subjected to many other linguistic influences. The Muslim invaders brought Arabic, Persian and Turkish. The British introduced English. The languages of the conquerors enriched the vocabulary of Punjabi without altering its basic structure. Since the Muslim invaders settled in Punjab, words of Arabic, Persian, and Turkish found their way into the language of the peasants. This did not apply to the same extent to English, which was restricted to matters of administration and technology and was used only by the educated classes.

GURMUKHI SCRIPT

Scholars still dispute the origin of the Gurmukhi script. The popular belief is that it was invented by the second Guru, Angad. This is, however, disproved by the fact that Guru Nanak used the thirty-five letters of the alphabet to compose his acrostic. From this some scholars have concluded that Nanak was the creator of Gurmukhi letters. Recently, documents written before the time of Nanak have been found which conclusively prove that the thirty-five letters of the alphabet (known also as the Painti, 35) now called Gurmukhi were in use a long time before the Gurus. Pritam Singh, whose authority is generally accepted, is of the opinion that Gurmukhi, like many other scripts in use in northern India, was derived from Brahmi letters which were in use at the time of Emperor Asoka (third century BCE), but no precise dates can be fixed about its evolution. Punjabi scholars (like the scholars of other languages) vie with each other in pushing back the antiquity of their literature. But there is little real evidence of Punjabi writing before the settlement of the Muslims in Punjab and the incorporation of their language in the local dialects. The earliest examples of the use of what may be described as Punjabi poetry were heroic ballads (yars) which were composed during the Muslim invasions. These heroic ballads were sung to specific tunes, many of which find mention in the compositions of Guru Nanak.

Early Punjabi writings were exclusively religious, being closely connected with the Bhakti movement (fifteenth to sixteenth centuries), of which the Sikh religion was itself an offshoot. The writers of this period fall into two main groups—the Sikh Gurus and Mussulman Sufis. They had much in common in their thought content, form and expression. Sufism was a revolt against the narrow bigotry of early Islam and insisted on the acceptance of certain Hindu doctrines.

The Bhakti movement, particularly Sikhism, was, on the other hand, a revolt against the anti-Muslim prejudices of the Hindus and demanded recognition of Islamic values. This resulted in the birth of a system of philosophy half-Islamic and half-Hindu. It also brought about a literature in which Arabic and Persian mixed with Sanskrit and Hindi with such facility that it became difficult to tell which language was basic and which the addition. This was the Punjabi of the Sikh Gurus and their contemporary Sufi writers.

THE SUFIS
Of the many Sufi orders in India, three flourished in Punjab and produced a crop of poets: the Chishtiya had Farid Shakarganj (twelfth century), the Qalandari, Shah Husain (sixteenth century) and the Qadiri Bulleh Shah, who was a contemporary of Guru Gobind Singh.

Some students of literature trace Punjabi literary writing to the twelfth century, to the works of Sheikh Farid Shakarganj. He was a disciple of the Sufi Saint Qutb-ud-din Bakhtiyar Kaki who lived in Mehrauli (Delhi). Over 130 of his compositions were incorporated into the Adi Granth by its compiler Guru Arjun and he was thus accorded a status equal to those of the ten Sikh Gurus. Farid Shakarganj is the first great name in Punjabi literature. He made his home in Pak Pattan, where his successors (who also took on the name Farid) continued to reside, write religious verse, and propagate Sufi doctrines. Consequently, there has been some controversy amongst scholars that the Farid in the Adi Granth is not Farid Shakarganj but his successor ,many generations removed, named Shaikh Ibrahim Farid who was a contemporary of Guru Nanak.

The first time I was attracted to Farid's poetry was on hearing Ragi Santa Singh's rendering of 'Jal jasee dhola hatth na laeen kusumrey' (Beloved, do not touch the kusum flower, it will burn your hands). It is a somewhat obscure poem warning people of wasting their lives in futile pastimes.

> When it was time to build your bark
> You did not try.
> When you see the ocean angry and the waves lash,
> For help you cry.
> Touch not the kusum flower, Beloved,
> It will burn your fingers.
> You are tender
> And the Master's words are harsh.
> As milk taken returns not to the udder,
> So a wasted life is without meeting with the Master.
> Says Farid: Sisters, when our husbands send for us, go we must.
> Our souls like swans fly away, our bodies come to dust.

A great favourite of Farid's is admonishing those who hold back from their tryst with the Beloved on flimsy grounds:

> O Farid, the lane is slushy with mud
> The house of the one thou lovest is far away,
> If thou goest, it will soak thy cloak

If thou stayest, it will sunder thy love.
I'll let my cloak be soaked.
'Tis Allah who makes the rain come down in torrents.
I will go forth to seek my Beloved
The bonds of our love will not sever.

We are not the only ones afflicted with sorrow, Farid reminds us:

Farid believed he alone was stricken with sorrow
But sorrow is spread over the entire world;
I climbed my roof and whichever way I turned
I saw that everyone is sorrow-burned.

It is not possible to say with certainty which of the many Farids was
the author of a particular line of a verse; 112 slokas ascribed to Farid
are incorporated in the Granth. Farid's chief preoccupation was with
death. He described himself 'lying on the bed of care on the mattress
of sorrow under the quilt of loneliness'; a strain of melancholy is
consequently present in much of his writing. In the tradition of the
Sufis and the Bhaktas, Farid wrote of a man's search for God in the
same terms as a woman's physical longing for her lover. (This tradition
was continued by the Sikh Gurus.)

Shah Husain of Lahore was given to drinking, music, dancing,
and pederasty. His eccentric ways as well as his verses were on people's
lips. Nothing of his writings remains except some hafts in mystic strain
which were recorded later. The strains of melancholy and abandon
run through most of the compositions ascribed to him. 'To whom
can I narrate the pain I suffer being separated from the Beloved? The
anguish has crazed my mind and my thinking. I have wandered from
forest to jungle looking for Him. Yet I have not found Him. The fire
smoulders: I search its embers and, through the black smoke, see my
Beloved. Sayeth the Faqir Husain, "Lord! behold the fate of those
stricken with love!"'

Bulleh Shah (1680–1758), born in a village near Kasur, remains
the most quoted and sung Sufi poet of Punjab. He became a disciple
of Inayat Shah of the Qadiri order, abandoned the mosque for the
Sufi dargah to sing songs of love. 'The first rung on love's ladder is

the limbo between life and death,' he wrote, 'when pilgrims turn to Mecca, I regard the face of my Beloved.'

In another verse he writes: 'The law says go to the Mullah to learn rules and regulations. Love says: one word is enough, put away your books of law. Law says: go and bathe five times and worship alone in the temple. Love replies: Your worship is false if you consider yourself separate from your Beloved.'

The Sufis lived in villages and their vocabulary was refreshingly rustic. The day-to-day activities of peasants, artisans and their womenfolk, the complicated emotional relationships between the various members of joint families—a sister's love for her brother, the tension between co-wives, the tyranny of a mother-in-law, etc.— gave them the similes and metaphors they needed. The Sikh Gurus, particularly Nanak, made use of these familiar pastimes and situations to convey their message.

Another notable contribution of the Sufis was the popularization of certain forms of verse which became distinctive of Punjabi literature, for example, the kafi, bara mah, and the siharfi. Kafi (a verse of four lines in which the first, second and the fourth are in rhyme) was well known to Persian poets and is popular today in Urdu verse. The bara mah, or the twelve months, gave poets full liberty to describe the beauty of the seasons and with that convey their message. Some of the richest descriptions of nature in Punjabi poetry owe their origin to the practice of composing bara mah. That of Guru Nanak in the Adi Granth is probably the most beautiful of all in the language. The siharfi, or the acrostic, takes a letter of the alphabet as its cue. This acrostic was used by the Sikh Gurus but was abandoned soon after them and never revived.

THE SIKH GURUS

Most of the Sikh Gurus were given to versification and the writings of Nanak, Angad, Amar Das, Ram Das, Arjun, and Tegh Bahadur are preserved in the Granth Sahib. The two outstanding contributors to the Sikh scriptures are the first Guru, Nanak, and the fifth Guru, Arjun.

Guru Nanak preached through his poetry, and consequently his works have a didacticism explaining his philosophy of life and exhorting others to a particular way of living. Most didactic poetry suffers from a cramping narrowness imposed by the purpose for which it is written, but Guru Nanak's poetry displays a remarkable freedom of expression. The beauty of pastoral Punjab, the ripening cornfields, the break of dawn, and the awakening of birds, the graceful flight of deer in the woodlands, the majesty of monsoon clouds and the music of rainfall— all aroused him to religious and poetic frenzy. The commonplace was for him pregnant with symbolism of moral significance.

Domestic situations, relations between husband and wife, and all the intricate relationships peculiar to the joint Hindu family, became his similes. Household duties of a rural home, gleaning of corn, picking of cotton, weaving and spinning, milking of cattle and churning of butter gave him his metaphors. The best known works of Guru Nanak are his *Babur Vani* (which also depicts the tyranny and lawlessness at the time of Babur's invasion), *Asa di War* (hymn of the morning) and Japji Sahib, the morning prayer.

The following three verses from the morning prayer are typical of his style:

As a beggar goes a-begging,
Bowl in one hand, staff in the other,
Rings in his ears, in ashes smothered,
So go thou forth in life.
With earrings made of contentment,
With modesty thy begging bowl,
Meditation the fabric of thy garment,
Knowledge of death thy cowl.
Let thy mind be chaste, virginal clean,
Faith the staff on which to lean.
Thou shalt then thy fancy humiliate
With mind subdued, the world subjugate.

Hail! and to Thee be salutation.
Thou art primal, Thou art pure,
Without beginning, without termination,
In single form, for ever endure.
(Verse 28)

From the storehouse of compassion,
Seek knowledge for thy food.
Let thy heartbeat be the call of the conch shell
Blown in gratitude.
He is the Lord, He is the Will, He is the creation,
He is the master of destiny, of union and separation.
Hail! and to thee be salutation.
Thou art primal, Thou art pure
Without beginning, without termination,
In single form, forever endure.
(Verse 29)

If thou must make a gold coin true
Let thy mint these rules pursue.
In the forge of continence
Let the goldsmith be a man of patience,
His tools be made of knowledge,
His anvil of reason;
With the fear of God the bellows blow,
With prayer and austerity make the fire glow.
Pour the liquid in the mould of love,
Print the name of the Lord thereon,
And cool it in the holy waters.
(Verse 38)

Guru Arjun's poetry expresses the same deep sentiments as Guru
Nanak's. His verse abounds with jewelled phrases and has a haunting
melody produced by the use of alliteration and repetition of words.
Sukhmani is Guru Arjun's greatest composition. The Granth is the
greatest work of Punjabi literature. Most of the labour involved in
its compilation was done by Guru Arjun and a contemporary writer,
Gurdas. It is a voluminous book containing nearly 6,000 verses.

Besides the writings of the six Gurus mentioned, it has in it selected
verses of several poet-saints associated with the Bhakti movement. Guru
Gobind Singh was perhaps the most erudite of all the Sikh Gurus and
was familiar with Hindu mythology as well as Islamic theology. He was
a patron of art and letters, and had fifty-two poets in his own court.

He wrote mainly in Sanskrit and Persian (and just one couplet in Punjabi). Unlike his predecessor, he did not restrict himself to expressing the glory of God in his verses. Guru Gobind Singh's writings have a moral as well as a political significance. The martial spirit which he infused amongst his followers is expressed in the vigorous poetry of his famous *Zafarnama*, the 'Epistle of Victory', addressed to Emperor Aurangzeb. His Jap Sahib is to this day a source of inspiration to his followers. Guru Gobind Singh's works were compiled and edited by his contemporary, Mani Singh.

The writing in the Adi Granth is the best that Punjabi literature has hitherto achieved. It has a form and finish not equalled by subsequent writers. The beauty of its composition has a powerful appeal, and large numbers of Punjabi Hindus read the Sikh scripture. The entire non-Muslim population of Sindh read and worship the Granth together with their own deities. After the passing of the ten Gurus, a spate of literature was produced on the lives of the Gurus by their contemporaries and others who were able to glean information on the subject. These biographies are known as 'Janam Sakhis' and are valuable historical records. The more well-known historians of the period were Seva Ram, Ram Koer, Santokh Singh, Ratan Singh Bhangu and Gyan Singh.

No literature was produced by the Sikhs during their struggle for power. But while they were busy fighting, two Muslims, Bulleh Shah (1680–1752) and Waris Shah (1735–1798), wrote verse which is the finest example of romantic and mystic Punjabi poetry. Bulleh Shah's *Kafis* and Waris Shah's epic *Heer Ranjah* are the most popular and are recited and sung in every village in the province. They have also influenced subsequent generations of Punjabi writers.

CONTEMPORARY PUNJABI WRITING
The starting point of contemporary Punjabi writing is Shah Mohammed (1784–1862) who, after Guru Nanak, was the first to write about events of his time. He witnessed the chaos that followed the death of Maharaja Ranjit Singh ending in the Anglo-Sikh wars and the annexation of the Sikh kingdom by the British. He immortalized the heroic but suicidal charge led by Sham Singh Attariwala in the battle

of Sabraon. 'They squeezed the blood of Whites as one squeezes juice out of a lemon,' he wrote. 'If only Ranjit Singh were there he would have been proud to see how his Khalsa wielded their swords.' He explained the outcome of the war in words which people still quote to this day:

O Shah Mohammad, without Ranjit, such was our plight
We won our battles, but lost the fight.

For nearly half a century following the commencement of British occupation, little literature was produced in India. It took many years to recover from the effects of the political change and to size up Western values. Early English rulers were convinced that all oriental culture was worthless and that the best thing the Indians could do was to adopt the European. One generation of Indians agreed with this opinion and anglicized themselves to the extent that they lost contact with Indian tradition and learning. The next generation discovered the folly and proceeded to blow away the dust of the archives housing the achievements of ancient India. This process took place all over the country. Since Punjab was the last to be subjected to Western complexes, it was the last to shake off their effect. The renaissance in Punjabi writing was consequently somewhat later than in the rest of the country. Post-annexation Punjabi writing corresponded roughly to the social and political changes produced by the Singh Sabha movement followed by the Akali and the Marxist. In each case, the literary output bore the impress of the problems which faced the protagonists of these movements. There were, however, some writers who remained oblivious to social and political problems and wrote, as it were, for the sake of writing.

THE SINGH SABHA MOVEMENT

The literary output of the Singh Sabha movement is the most important part of its contribution to Sikhism. The person to whom it owes most is Bhai Vir Singh, who recreated interest in Punjabi and established a landmark in the history of the language. Vir Singh wrote fiction, poetry (notably ghazals) and commentaries on the sacred texts. Vir Singh's early writing has to be viewed with reference to the social and political conditions at the end of the nineteenth century. His novels, which made him known in millions of homes, were written at a time when Punjabis were beginning to doubt the achievements of their ancestors. English historians harped on the crude and corrupt Sikh rule, which they had replaced by an 'enlightened' one. Sanskrit scholars belittled the religion of the Sikhs as a poor imitation of the Vedic and ridiculed its forms and symbols as barbarous. Vir Singh's novels, *Sundari, Vijay Singh, Satwant Kaur* and *Baba Naudh Singh,* had as their central theme the heroism and chivalry of the Sikhs and the ethical excellence of their religion. This was set in contrast to the servility of the Hindu masses and the oppression of the Pathan and Mughal rulers. The Sikhs devoured Vir Singh's novels with enthusiasm and gratitude. But with the passing of that peculiar mental state, the novels lost their appeal. To the present-day reader, they appear somewhat insipid. Their place is not in literature but in history. Vir Singh himself gave up writing fiction and turned to translating and explaining the scriptures in a series of pamphlets and in his weekly paper, the *Khalsa Samachar.* Along with these appeared his poems, which gave him the most honoured place amongst Punjabi poets.

Vir Singh first experimented in blank verse. A long poem, *Rana Surat Singh,* was published in 1905. The theme, as usual, was religion. His technique and mastery over the language was impressive. No one had successfully written blank verse in Punjabi before; Vir Singh turned out a work of sustained excellence, where alliteration and onomatopoeia, rhythm, and repetition produced a lilting melody with all the languorous sensuousness of a summer afternoon. Thereafter Vir Singh wrote the biographies of two Sikh Gurus, the founder, Nanak, and the last, Guru Gobind Singh. *Kalgidhar Chamatkar,* the life of Guru Gobind, appeared first and was followed three years later by *Guru Nanak Chamatkar.* The lives of the remaining eight Gurus were composed in *Asht Guru Chamatkar.*

In between these biographies, Vir Singh published several collections of verse employing a short metre not used by Punjabi poets. The most popular of these were in the form of rubayas (familiar to the readers of Omar Khayyam). In these he expressed his philosophy and mysticism, where the love of God and human beings, the spiritual and the sensual, moral and divine, moved in a colourful kaleidoscope, beautiful and baffling. There was always an underlying sense of humility, at times almost masochistic. Bhai Vir Singh did not give up experimenting even in his later years. In *The Vigil,* published posthumously, he recaptured his ability to describe nature and invest physical longing with divine attributes:

Shades of twilight fell,
A gentle gloom had spread.
I mused: maybe today
You would come when it was dark.
I blew out the street lamp,
Put out the light in the niche,
Smothered the taper in the house.

I sat in the dark and was lost in waiting
Maybe tonight
You might wish to come
With soft, unsounding tread,
In absolute stillness, in absolute dark.

◆

Hark! What was that noise?
Was He coming?
I went and looked out of my window,
There was lightning and thunder.

My heart stopped.
Maybe tonight
You might come
With fireworks
And with flaming torches!

I rose in a hurry,
Put on the light in the house,
Touched with flame the taper in the niche,
Relit the lamp in the street
With eager, impatient haste.

I mused: Maybe
You would come seeing the light,
Maybe you would turn back if the house were in darkness
And I be left waiting for ever and ever.

◆

Clouds gathered, black and lowering,
Torn by flashes of lightning,
Then came rain in torrents,
Lanes and streets became muddy swamps.

The lightning is over,
Gone in a flicker of an eyelid
As if it knew my heart's desire.
Even the dark clouds are gone
Baring a sky clean-washed and shining,
Carrying the moon in its lap like a babe
With the stars scattered around.
Still I sit and wait.

The moon also awaits.
Look, how the moonbeams have spread
Their shimmering silver over the mud,
Spread a carpet of velvet-white on Your path!

◆

The first ray of dawn has lit the sky,
The sparrow twitters,
The morning breeze,
Soft, sweet, fluting,
Enfolds me in its embrace.
Great Giver! Light of the Morning!
Everything, everywhere wakes to life,
Expectant are dawn and daylight.

The longing burgeons with the morning.
The sun is risen

As yesterday it rose and every day.
People have woken from their slumbers
And go about the streets and by-lanes.
Only I sit and wait.
Lord, what else can I do!
Lord, what more can I do!

Two contemporaries of Bhai Vir Singh, Puran Singh (1881–1931) and Dhani Ram 'Chatrik' (1870–1954) deserve mention. Puran Singh, trained in chemistry in which he submitted several research papers, turned to creative literature in Punjabi and English. He was influenced by Walt Whitman and produced some vigorous blank verse in both languages. Whereas Bhai Vir Singh was a traditionalist and extolled the golden past of the Sikhs, Puran Singh was forward looking, emphasized the Sikhs' Punjabi identity, the universality in the writings of the Sikh Gurus and the role of the self in moulding human destiny. His better known works in English are *Sisters of the Spinning Wheel, Path of Life* and *Spirit Born People.*

Dhani Ram 'Chatrik' published several collections of verse. His lyrics were surfeit with Punjabi colloquialisms—charming in the original but extremely hard to translate. Poetry remains the most popular form of literary expression to this day. Newspapers and magazines devote a large part of their space to poems, and a symposium (kavi darbar) will still draw a larger crowd than a political or a religious meeting. Most of this new poetry is, however, of indifferent quality. Two exceptions are Mohan Singh and Amrita Pritam.

Mohan Singh (1905–78) made a promising start with his *Saave Patr* (Green Leaves) and soon came to be recognized as the best of the younger poets. His later work, published after Partition, showed a strong left-wing bias, where political emotion was given precedence over poetical form—a malaise which has afflicted a large number of younger writers who label themselves 'progressive'. In the case of Mohan Singh, the first flush of Marxism soon settled down to simple championing of the underdog and an exhortation to work. He was once more able to recapture the spontaneous beauty of his earlier writing:

The pitch-black within the pitcher has burst
Spilling the milk-white of the moonlight.
It is time we talked of a new dawn
And gave up the gossiping of the night.

I grant that autumn's touch
Hath robbed some leaves of their sap.
Sorrow not for what is lost and gone,
With hope anew fill thy lap.

How long on the ancient vault of heaven
Idle fantasies draw and hold them dear?
Come let us caress the earth's tresses,
Come let us talk of something near.

Amrita Pritam published her first collection of poems when she was only seventeen. Her earliest efforts were heavy with criticism of evil social customs. Although she gave up preaching, the hard lot of Indian women remained the dominant theme in most of her poetry and prose. Her writing improved steadily as the songstress in her gained dominance over the suffragette, but the feminist protest was never totally silenced. She was influenced by her pseudo-Marxist contemporaries, became 'progressive' and at times propagandist. The great famine of Bengal of 1943 moved her to declaim that 'the talk of love and beauty is talk of idle times and idle people'. But once again the mother in her triumphed over the Marxist and her writing took the form of a soulful dirge rather than an angry denunciation. She became in her own words, 'the chronicler of India's misfortunes'. The internecine massacres of 1947, which took such a heavy toll of human life, stirred her to write one of her most memorable poems. She addressed it to Waris Shah and exhorted him to rise from his grave and see the havoc wrought in his own land.

O, comforter of the sorrowing, rise and behold thy Punjab
Its fields are strewn with corpses, blood runs in the Chenab.

Amrita Pritam's poetry began veering towards the sentimental and romantic, with delicate allusions to natural phenomena:

Spring is here again,
Flowers are silken clad
For the festival of colours,
But thou are not here.

The days have lengthened,
The grape is touched with pink,
The scythe hath kissed the corn,
But thou art not here.

Clouds are spread across the sky,
The earth hath opened her palms
And drunk the draught of kindness,
But thou art not here.

The trees are touched with magic,
Lips of the winds that kiss the woodlands
Are full of honey,
But thou art not here.

Bewitching seasons have come and gone,
Many moons have woven plaits
On the black tresses of night,
But thou are not here.

Today again the stars did stay
In life's mansion, even now
The lamps of beauty are still aflame,
But thou art not here.

Rays of sun did also whisper,
In the deep slumbers of the night
The moon is ever awake,
But thou art not here.

Amrita Pritam did not achieve the same distinction in her fiction as
she did in her poetry. Her characterization was often weak and her
plots so contrived as to appear manifestly unreal. The Indian film
industry has exercised on her, as it has on many Indian writers of her

generation, a most baneful influence—the narratives of their novels are interspersed with song, and people find themselves in situations which we seldom come across in real life in India.

A contemporary of Mohan Singh and Amrita Pritam was the revolutionary agnostic poet Darshan Singh. Since he intended to communicate with the illiterate masses, his poems were propagandist and meant to be recited at political gatherings. Of a different genre is Harbhajan Singh who distinguished himself by use of new diction and lyricism. His better known works include *Adhraini* (Midnight) and *Na Dhuppe Na Chhaven* (Neither in Sunshine Nor in Shade).

Two poets deserve mention as trendsetters for the modern generation of writers: Tara Singh Kamil, a carpenter by profession, also representative of the reaction to obscurantism which had at one time come into vogue. He is a favourite of the kavi darbars, where rapport between the bard and his audience is essential. *The Lovers' Plight* is a sample of his technique:

> In the months of May and June.
> In the summer's heat, on a hot afternoon,
> Like a fluff of thistledown floating in the air
> Casting its shadow on a piece of straw
> For a fleeting moment; so hath
> Thy love been to me.
>
> Beloved mine! Thy face is like the moon
> New risen in the hours of early dawn.
> I have treasured the memory of thy love
> As traveller numb and cold
> Seeks shelter in the wayside hut, and
> When rain and sleet beat upon its thatched roof
> He lights a fire, guards the glowing embers
> In his embrace and lets the dirty water
> Leaking through the roof drip upon his back,
> So have I cherished thy love.

Shiv Kumar Batalvi burst on the Punjabi literary scene like a meteor. He was a raffish young man with his roots in the dung heaps of his village and steeped in folklore and mythology. He was a poet; whatever he wrote turned into a lyrical masterpiece. His best known work, *Loona*, was based on the story of Prince Pooran Bhagat, son of King Salvathan. In the epic, the prince rejects his stepmother's (Loona's) advances. Feeling insulted, she instigates her old husband to torture his son for having coveted her. In Shiv Batalvi's version, Loona, instead of being the villain, is depicted as a lusty young woman frustrated by her ageing husband's impotence and yearning for love from her handsome stepson. *Loona* won immediate acclaim. Shiv Batalvi was the youngest writer to have been given the Sahitya Akademi Award in 1967. He drank himself to death before he was thirty-seven. 'The best time to die is in the fullness of youth,' he wrote.

BELLES LETTRES, FICTION, AND DRAMA

The outstanding figures in Punjabi prose are Gurbaksh Singh, editor of the monthly magazine *Prit Lahri*, and Dr Balbir Singh, younger brother of the poet Vir Singh. Gurbaksh Singh was closely associated with the Communist Party and had been the main influence on many of Punjab's younger writers. His manifestly propagandist writing was, however, redeemed by a felicity of style and diction. Gurbaksh Singh wrote novels, plays, short stories, and essays. Dr Balbir Singh was, like his brother, deeply religious; he was also the most erudite of contemporary Sikh writers. His essays display a knowledge of both European and Sanskrit literature and are written in chaste and simple Punjabi. He published two books *Kalam di Karaamaat* (The Miracle of the Pen) and *Lami Nadar* (Grace Abounding)—both of which were acclaimed by critics.

The novel as a form of writing came somewhat late to Punjab. The best known contemporary novelist, Nanak Singh, wrote over two dozen novels and remains the most widely-read Punjabi writer. His language is of the less educated class of Indians and is interspersed with English words; his plots are contrived.

Punjabi literature's most notable achievement is in its short stories. By introducing modern techniques, the Punjabi writer has been able to develop the tradition of the fable. Sant Singh Sekhon abandoned the straightforward narrative and made dexterous use of illusion, understatement, and auto-suggestion. Kartar Singh Duggal is the leading writer of short stories and introduced the dialect of Rawalpindi district into Punjabi writing. His collections *Sver Sar* (Early Morning) and *Navaan Ghar* (New Home) are noteworthy. In the same way Kulwant Singh Virk injected the dialect of the Jats of Majha into his short stories. Virk's later work became somewhat sophisticated and he began to write of the lower middle-class life in small towns.

A significant modernization in the style of short-story writing has come with the emergence of Ajeet Cour. Several dozen or so novelettes and collections of short stories have been translated into English, Urdu and Hindi and published in prestigious journals. In her work is brevity, wit, satire and subdued pathos without any indulgence in hyperbole or purple prose. For the first time we get a candid exposure of human emotions and physical relationships. Her autobiography *Khanabdosh* (Homeless Wanderer) tells of her broken marriage, the death of her younger child and the struggle for survival of a young divorcee in a venally masculine society. It won her the Sahitya Akademi Award in 1986.

The most neglected aspect of Punjabi writing is drama. Punjabi dramatists' exposition has been confined to writing plays for broadcasting or suffering them to be performed by amateurs at drama festivals. Nevertheless, Balwant Gargi had some of his plays translated and enacted in the Soviet Union, and United States, Canada and on TV.

BARA MAH

Composing verses on the twelve months of the year was once common amongst Indian poets. It gave them the opportunity to describe nature and human moods, and moralize at the same time. Several exist in the Punjabi language, of which Guru Nanak's is the most highly rated. It is believed to be amongst the last of the Guru's compositions.

CHET (MARCH–APRIL)
Chet basant bhala bhavar suhavde
>It is the month of Chet
>It is spring. All is seemly,
>The humming bumblebees
>The woodlands in flower;
>But there is sorrow in my soul
>For the Lord my Master is away
>If the husband comes not home, how can a wife
>Find peace of mind?
>Sorrows of separation waste away her body.
>The koel calls in the mango grove,
>Her notes are full of joy
>But there is sorrow in my soul.
>The bumblebee hovers about the blossoming bough
>(A messenger of life and hope)
>But O mother of mine, 'tis like death to me
>For there is sorrow in my soul.
>How shall I banish sorrow and find blessed peace?
>Sayeth Nanak: When the Lord her Master comes home to her
>Then is spring seemly because she is fulfilled.

VAISAKH (APRIL–MAY)

Vaisakh bhala sakha ves kare

Beauteous Vaisakh, when the bough adorns itself anew
The wife awaits the coming of her Lord
Her eyes fixed on the door.
'My love, who alone can help me cross
The turbulent waters of life,
Have compassion for me and come home,
Without thee I am as worthless as a shell.
Love, look thou upon me with favour
And let our eyes mingle
Then I will become priceless beyond compare.'
Nanak asks: 'Whither seekest thou the Lord?
Whom awaitest thou?
Thou hast not far to go,
For the Lord is within thee,
Thou art His mansion.
If thy body and soul yearn for the Lord,
The Lord shall love thee
And Vaisakh will beautiful be.'

JETH (MAY–JUNE)

Mah jeth bhala pritam kyon bisrai

Why forget the Lord in the month of Jeth
When the earth shimmers in the summer's heat?
The wife makes obeisance and prays
Let me find favour in Thine eyes O Lord,
Thou art great and good
Truth manifest and unshakable,
Of attachments art Thou free.
And I, lowly, humble, helpless.
How shall I approach Thee?
How find the haven of peace?
In the month of Jeth, says Nanak,
She who knoweth the Lord
Becometh like the Lord.
She knoweth Him

By treading the path of virtue.

ASADH (JUNE–JULY)

Asadh bhala suraj gagan tapai

In Asadh the sun scorches.
Skies are hot
The earth burns like an oven
Waters give up their vapours.
It burns and scorches relentlessly
Thus the land fails not
To fulfil its destiny.
The sun's chariot passes the mountain tops;
Long shadows stretch across the land
And the cicada calls from the glades.
The beloved seeks the cool of the evening.
If the comfort she seeks be in falsehood,
There will be sorrow in store for her.
If it be in truth,
Hers will be a life of joy everlasting.
My life and its ending depend on the will of the Lord.
To Him, says Nanak, I surrendered my soul.

SAVAN (JULY–AUGUST)

Savan saras mana ghan varsai rut ae

O my heart, rejoice! It's Savan
The season of nimbus clouds and rain,
My body and soul yearn for my Lord.
But my Lord is gone to foreign lands.
If He return not, I shall die pining for Him.
The lightning strikes terror in my heart.
I stand all alone in my courtyard,
In solitude and in sorrow.
O mother of mine, I stand on the brink of death,
Without the Lord I have neither hunger nor sleep
I cannot suffer the clothes on my body.
Nanak says, she alone is the true wife
Who loses herself in the Lord.

BHADON (AUGUST–SEPTEMBER)

Bhadon bharam bhuli bhar joban pachtani

In the month of Bhadon
I lose myself in a maze of falsehood
I waste my wanton youth.
River and land are one endless expanse of water
For it is the monsoon, the season of merry-making.
It rains,
The nights are dark,
What comfort is it to the wife left alone?
Frogs croak
Peacocks scream
The papeeha calls 'peeoh, peeoh'.
The fangs of serpents that crawl,
The stings of mosquitoes that fly
Are full of venom.
The seas have burst their bounds in the ecstasy
Of fulfilment.
Without the Lord I alone am bereft of joy,
Whither shall I go?
Says Nanak, ask the Guru the way
He knoweth the path which leads to the Lord.

ASAN (SEPTEMBER–OCTOBER)

Asan au pira sa dhan jhur mui

It's the month of Asan
O Master come to me
I waste and I shall die. If the Master wills,
I shall meet Him.
If He wills not,
In a deep well shall I be lost.
I strayed on to the path of falsehood
And the Master forsook me.
Age hath greyed my locks
I have left many winters behind.
But the fires of hell still lie ahead.
Whither shall I turn?

The bough remaineth ever green
For the sap that moveth within day and night,
Night and day, reneweth life.
If the name of the Lord courseth in thy veins,
Life and hope will forever be green.
That which cooketh slowly cooketh best.
It is Asan, says Nanak,
It is trysting time, O Lord,
And we have waited long.

KATAK (OCTOBER–NOVEMBER)

Katak kirat paiya jo prabh bhaia

In the month of Katak
Will I get my due.
What pleases the Lord
Is all I merit.
The lamp of wisdom burneth steadily
If the oil that feeds it
Be reality.
If the oil that feeds the lamp
Be love,
The beloved will meet the Lord and be fulfilled.
Full of faults, she dies not
Nor gains release
It's death after virtuous life.
That doth the Lord please.
Those who are granted the worship of Thy name
Merge in Thee, for Thou art then
Their aim and end in life.
Nanak says: Lord, till Thou grant Your vision
And burst the bonds of superstition,
One watch of day will drag on like half a year.

MAGHAR (NOVEMBER–DECEMBER)

Maghar mah bhala harigun ank samave

The month of Maghar is bliss
For her who is lost in the Lord.

She singeth songs of joy and fulfilment.
Why not love the Lord who is eternal?
He who is eternal, wise, omniscient is also the master of destiny.
The world is agitated because it hath lost faith in Him.
She that hath knowledge and contemplates on Him,
Loses herself in Him.
She loveth the Lord, the Lord loveth her.
In song and dance and verse, let it be the name of Lord Rama
And sorrows will fly away.
Nanak says, only she is loved by her Lord
Who prayeth, not only with her lips
But worships Him with her soul.

POKH (DECEMBER–JANUARY)
Pokh tukhar pade van trin ras sokhai
As in the month of Pokh
Winter's frost doth freeze
The sap in tree and bush, so does
The absence of the Lord
Kill the body and the soul.
O Lord, why cometh not Thou?
I praise though the Guru's Word.
He that gives life to all the world,
His light shines in all life born
Of egg or womb or sweat or seed.
Merciful God and master! Thy vision grant
And grant me salvation.
Nanak says, only she mingles with Him
Who loves the Lord, the giver of life.

MAGH (JANUARY–FEBRUARY)
Magh punit bhai tirath antar jania
In the month of Magh
I made my ablution,
The Lord entered my being.
I made pilgrimage within myself and was purified.
I met Him.

He found me good
And let me lose myself in Him.
'Beloved! If Thou findest me fair
My pilgrimage is made,
My ablution done.
More than the sacred waters
Of Ganga, Yamuna and Triveni mingled at the Sangam,
More than the seven seas.
All these and charity, alms-giving and prayer,
Are the knowledge of eternity that is the Lord.'
Nanak says, Magh is the essence of ambrosia
For him who hath worshipped the great giver of life.
Hath done more than bathe in the sixty and eight places of
pilgrimage.

PHALGUN (FEBRUARY–MARCH)
Phalgun mah rahsi prem subhayae
In the month of Phalgun
She whose heart is full of love
Is ever in full bloom.
Day and night she is in spiritual exaltation
She is in bliss because she hath no love of self.
Only those that love Thee
Conquer love of self.
Be kind to me
And make my home Thy abode.
Many a lovely garment did I wear.
The Master willed not and
His palace doors were barred to me.
When He wanted me I went
With garlands and strings of jewels and raiments of finery.
O Nanak, a bride welcomed in the Master's mansion
Hath found her true Lord and Love.

NO ONE WILL GO HUNGRY

Many years ago Parveen Talha, the senior-most Muslim woman in the IAS and the big boss of Customs and Excise posted in Aurangabad, told me of a strange experience. She said, 'You know for some months every train at every stop on the way to Nanded (Maharashtra) has young Sardars entering all compartments to serve dal and roti to passengers free of charge. The dal is delicious. Who are these people?' I did not know but I told her that Nanded was one of the five takhts (thrones) of the Khalsa Panth; it has a huge gurdwara commemorating the assassination of their last Guru, Guru Gobind Singh, in 1708. I was intrigued and also happy that I belonged to the community of dal-roti servers.

A few weeks later, Mrs Charanjit Singh, who lives in New Friends Colony, told me: 'Every morning I go to my office in Le Meridien (she is chairman of the hotel), my car is held up near the dargah of Hazrat Nizamuddin Auliya because of a mob of hungry beggars milling round trucks loaded with dal-roti and rice which is distributed to them by a few young Sardars. I don't know who they are but I know most of the crowd consists of local Muslims or Bangladeshis.' I was more intrigued and asked her to find out who was organizing this free Guru ka Langar by the roadside. The next day, she rang me up and told me, 'It is someone known as Sant Tarlochan Singh.' She gave me his telephone number.

I got Sant Tarlochan Singh on the phone. 'I don't want any publicity,' he told me bluntly. 'It takes away any merit you may gain through sewa (service).' I persisted. 'You did not ring me up. I rang you. I want to know more about you and what you do.' He relented but put off the meeting because he had fractured his leg while starting a langar-cum-clinic at Bareilly for bonded labourers working in brick kilns. A week later, he was able to move with the use of a walker and came to see me with his son Kamaljeet Singh, a strapping young man in his mid-thirties.

Tarlochan Singh was sixty-seven, a tall man dressed in white from his turban, kurta, down to the pyjamas. He had a silken white beard flowing to his navel. He looked every inch a sant. 'I don't like to be called a sant, I prefer to be known as veerjee (elder brother),' he said with a broad smile. His residence was known as Veerjee Da Dera but his ashram was known as Santgarh (sant's fortress). It was here that cooking of large quantities of rice, dal and chapatis started every evening and rounded off by the early hours of next morning. It was then transported by trucks to different parts of the city and Delhi railway station. The queue outside Sis Ganj extended half a mile on either side. Veerjee himself would set out, broom in hand, on a round of the city's gurdwaras to sweep floors and say his prayers. I asked what had inspired him to undertake his mission to feed the hungry. Without hesitation he replied, 'Mother Teresa. I came to look upon her as my own mother and wanted to follow her example.'

Tarlochan Singh had many turns and twists in his life. He was born in Mandalay (Burma) in 1935, the son of a prosperous timber contractor. Mandalay was bombed by the Japanese in 1942. He saw his own sister killed by shrapnel. The family migrated back to their ancestral village in Ludhiana district. Tarlochan did his matriculation from his village school, went on to Government College, Ludhiana, for a degree in engineering and joined Punjab Works Department. In 1962, he was posted as an overseer in Delhi and was at the Pusa Agricultural Institute. He retired in 1998. Eight years before his retirement, he started on his mission to feed the poor. It became a full-time occupation. 'Where the poor are taken care of, there is Thy grace seen,' he said, quoting Guru Nanak on the existence of God. 'He fills pitchers that are empty and empties pitchers that are full.'

'Where does the money for this massive operation come from?' I asked. He raised both his hands and replied, 'God gives all I ask for.' This is exactly how Mother Teresa had answered the same question when I put it to her. Mother Teresa had the Missionaries of Charity to which anyone could make his or her donation. Tarlochan Singh has no such organization and bluntly refuses to take money from anyone. 'If you want to give anything, give me atta (flour), rice, dal or medicines,' he replied. His son Kamaljeet Singh who is a jewellery designer by profession promised to give me a list of medicines they needed. When would I have had the time to go and buy medicines in bulk and deliver them at Santgarh or Veerjee Da Dera, God alone knows. In any event no list was sent to me. God, who provided Tarlochan Singh with rations for the poor, now also provides medicines for the sick. He tends to them himself; his clinic was the pavement beside the Chandni Chowk entrance of Gurdwara Sis Ganj.

Both tehzeeb and etiquette are outdated concepts. One rarely hears any comments on saleega (can't think of an English equivalent) in the manner of speech. But foreigners often complain that we Indians lack manners. We don't say 'please' and 'thank you', our behaviour in public places is inconsiderate towards others and we are loud-mouthed. I am inclined to agree with the verdict, with the caveat that like the French we attach more importance to courtesy than to deportment. A Frenchman will kiss a lady's hand and pay the plainest looking girl the handsomest compliments. An Indian will touch another's feet when he would really like to kick him on the posterior, and shower words of praise on the least praiseworthy.

However, encounters between Indians and foreigners and their attempts to outdo each other in effusions of goodwill can often be amusing. I recount two incidents from my past.

A French lady was dining with a Sikh family consisting of many brothers who looked very much alike in their turbans and beards. The hostess introduced the eldest and the youngest, and, having nothing better to say, asked the visitor who she thought was the younger of the brothers. The French lady scrutinized the two from all angles like a connoisseur examines a work of art. Then she placed her finger on the younger man and explained with the necessary hesitation, 'I zink he is ze younger. But very, very little, only by about seex mons.'

When the hostess explained that the process of creation took a little longer in India, the guest was embarrassed. She was French and a Frenchwoman is expected to know the facts of life better than women of any other country. 'Mais oui oui,' she explained, recovering her composure. 'What are a few months this way or that, but we should always be polite, tojours la politesse n'est ce pas?'

The Americans have an altogether fresh approach to the problem of human relationships. Good manners and courtesy are charmingly old-worldly but they do not get one anywhere. One has to get around a person, and to do that one should know the other's name (and use it as often as possible), know office problems and interests, discuss them and generally flatter his ego into utter submission. The technique can misfire. I recall meeting an American lady who had risen to dizzy heights of social success by mastering her Dale Carnegie. Before she met me, she had taken the trouble to find out something of my antecedents and consulted the Encyclopaedia Britannica on the Sikhs. She communicated this information to me. Having fed my vanity and aroused my interest, she lapsed into an indifferent silence—broken by two sentences she repeated alternately at suitable intervals. The conversation proceeded somewhat as follows:

'I've been reading about your community, the Sikhs. Violent lot, aren't they? I wonder why?'

I explained how virile people are often violent and Sikhs were a very virile race.

'How nice.'

It wasn't nice at all, I continued, because they could do so much that was constructive. The Sikh peasant wasted a lot of energy in being violent.

'I wonder why?'

Family feuds, odd notions of honour, sometimes just to crack a bald skull for the fun of it.

'How nice.'

It wasn't nice at all, I insisted. Marxists believe that the ultimate cause of crime is poverty and here was India's richest peasantry with the highest incidence of violence.

'I wonder why?'

I went over the business of family feuds and vendettas again. I also explained that the Sikh peasants did not stoop to anything as low as petty pilfering or robbery. But when it came to fighting, they were like the Irish. 'Would you believe,' I said in a tone of horror, 'that of every ten chaps hanged for murder in Punjab at least nine will be Sikhs.'

'Oh, how nice.'

It was the winter of 1947 and late in the evening. The sky was overcast and a fine drizzle fell on the deserted street. A cold wind blew and chilled my bones. I wrapped my thick overcoat closer to my body. The boy who sat huddled alongside the wall of the shop hugging a bundle of newspapers was wearing a cotton shirt and pyjamas. He was barely ten years old. He was a Sikh but had no turban to cover his topknot nor shoes on his feet. He shivered in the cold. I could hear his teeth rattle.

'Give me the evening paper,' I said and handed him a rupee note.

He stood up and handed me the paper. Then he began to undo the knot in the hem of his shirt in which he had tied up his change. He was a delicately built child with light brown hair. His long eyelashes curved up towards his eyebrows like a film star's. It was obvious he came from a well-to-do urban family.

'Keep the change,' I said in as gentle a manner as I could. I expected him to get embarrassed with gratitude. Instead, he turned on me like an angry baby cobra. He snatched the paper out of my hand and flung the rupee note on the ground. 'You think I am a beggar!' he hissed indignantly. He picked up his bundle of papers and disappeared into the night.

That little Sikh boy symbolized the indomitable spirit of the people of Punjab. Five million of them were compelled to leave their homes, lands and shops in Pakistan a few months after Partition. These five million included the landed gentry, some of whom owned estates of the richest canal-irrigated lands of India yielding almost a lakh of rupees a month. After Partition they contented themselves with a few miserable acres of thorn and shrub without any irrigation facilities. There were eminent lawyers and doctors with well-established practices who had to rebuild their homes, libraries, laboratories and clinics in strange towns and cities. There were petty tradesmen who had to start their small businesses from scratch. Above all, there was the peasantry which had once more to clear jungles, drain marshes and turn the sod on virgin lands. One saw schoolgirls abandon their books to ply tongas. One saw erstwhile owners of industry hawking goods on the streets. They grumbled a little—but never was a hand stretched out to ask for alms.

Do you know how much our Punjabis lost in this exchange of population?

Our people who came out of West Pakistan left 21,448 square kilometres of land. People who left India and went to Pakistan left behind 15,580 square kilometres acres of land. So we were short by 5,868 square kilometres of land. Our loss in residential property was even worse. Our people left behind in Pakistan property worth Rs 500 crore. Property left by migrants to Pakistan was worth less than Rs 100 crore i.e. less than a fifth.

To this day Pakistan has not paid a single anna to compensate for the difference.

The people of Punjab have, however, rehabilitated themselves by their own resources and the generous help given to them by their government. The tragic tale of Punjab is over.

The refugee problem of Bengal is unlike the one in Punjab. The migrations in Punjab were finished once and for all when all the non-Muslims were ejected from West Pakistan. Our government at least knew what it was up against. The migration of Hindus from East Pakistan continues. Of the 12 million Hindus in 1947 only 8 million remain today. And even now they keep coming over, sometimes in trickles of twos and fours; then suddenly in the thousands. We cannot plan ahead, and each wave of immigrants causes a crisis. In Punjab, the movement was a two-way traffic. Refugees who came to India found lands and homes—however inadequate—left by those who left India. In Bengal it is a one-way traffic—from Pakistan to India. (Ours is a secular democracy wedded to Mahatma Gandhi's principles of keeping India the home of all religions and races without any discrimination—so our minorities are safe and happy in their homes.) West Bengal was densely populated and now its capacity to take refugees has reached bursting point. To add to these difficulties, there is the reluctance of the Bengalis to settle in areas other than those where Bengali is spoken.

◆

Amongst the greatest achievements of our government in the ten years of its existence is the resettlement of refugees from Pakistan. And it has done so without putting out the begging bowl to any foreign power or agency. Almost all the 5 million refugees from Punjab have found homes and means of living. The same process is taking place in Bengal now. Today, there are 350,000 displaced persons living in 211 camps. Many thousand others have been put to work in hydroelectric projects, digging canals and making roads provided for in our Five-Year Plan. There are 351 settlements for refugees in the state. New townships, new schools, colleges and technical training centres have sprung up everywhere. Anyone travelling in West Bengal today will be struck by the enormous amount of work done in rebuilding new cities and adding to the old ones.

All this has taken a heavy toll on our development programmes. We have already spent Rs 300 crore on these resettlement schemes. In addition, we continue to spend Rs 3 lakh every day for the immediate needs of the refugees in West Bengal.

One has mixed feelings on the subject of refugees. On the one hand there is the feeling of pride in the great achievement. On the other, one of sorrow: how much bigger would our economy and prosperity have been if we did not have to spend so much money and energy on the rehabilitation of displaced persons.

PART II
MY BLEEDING PUNJAB

VILLAGE IN THE DESERT

It is safest to begin with the beginning.

Where I was born I have been told by people who were present at my birth. When I was born remains a matter of conjecture. I am told I was born in a tiny hamlet called Hadali, lost in the sand dunes of the Thar Desert some thirty kilometres west of the River Jhelum and somewhat the same distance southward of the Khewra Salt Range. Hadali is now deep inside Pakistan. At the time I was born, my father, Sobha Singh, was away in Delhi with his father, Sujan Singh. When the news was sent to him, he did not bother to put it down in his diary. I was his second son. At that time, records of births and deaths were not kept in our villages. Unlike Hindus who noted down the time of birth of their offspring so that their horoscopes could be cast, we Sikhs had no faith in astrology, and therefore attached no importance to the time and place of nativity. Several years later, when he had to fill a form for our admission to Modern School in Delhi, my father gave my elder brother's and my date of birth out of his imagination. Mine was put down as 2 February 1915. Years later, my grandmother told me that I was born in Badroo—sometime in August. I decided to fix it in the middle of the month, to 15 August 1915, and made myself a Leo. Thirty-two years later, in 1947, 15 August became the birthday of independent India.

Sometime after I had been weaned, my father came to Hadali to take my mother and elder brother to Delhi, where he and his father had secured some building contracts. I was left with my grandmother. For the first few years of my life she was my sole companion and friend. Her name I later discovered was Lakshmi Bai. We called her Bhaabeejee. Like her, my mother also had a Hindu—Maharashtrian—name: Veeran Bai. The children knew her as Baybayjee.

117

I have hazy recollections of my childhood years in Hadali. The village consisted of about three hundred families, most of them Muslims of Baluch extraction. They were enormous men, mostly serving in the British Indian Army, or having retired from it. A fair proportion of the viceroy's bodyguard came from Hadali. Till recently, a marble plaque on a wall alongside the railway station master's office stated that Hadali had provided proportionately more soldiers from its population for World War I than any other village in India. There were about fifty Hindu and Sikh families engaged in trade, shopkeeping and moneylending. My ancestors—I can only trace them back to my great-grandfather, Inder Singh, and his father, Pyare Lal, who converted to Sikhism and became Sohel Singh—were tradesmen. They had camel caravans which took rock salt from the Khewra mines, and dates, the only fruit of our desert homeland, to sell in Lahore and Amritsar. They brought back textiles, kerosene oil, tea, sugar, spices and other items to sell in neighbouring towns and villages. Later, my grandfather and father got into the construction business. They laid a part of the small-gauge rail track and tunnels on the Kalka-Simla railway.

We were the most prosperous family of Hadali. We lived in a large brick-and-mud house with a spacious courtyard enclosing a buffalo shed and had a well of our own. The entrance was a massive wooden door that was rarely opened. It had a small aperture to let people in. A number of Hindus and Sikhs served us as clerks, and hired Muslim camel drivers took our wares to the markets. Many Muslim families were our debtors.

Our family's prosperity was ascribed to a legend. It is said that one year, when it rained heavily on the Salt Range, floodwaters swept down the rocky ridge, carrying with them a Muslim holy man named Shaida Peer who had climbed on to the thatched roof of his hut. By the time he floated down to Hadali, he had nothing on him except his loincloth. My grandfather, Sujan Singh, gave him clothes, made a hut for him near the Muslim graveyard and sent him food. Shaida Peer blessed him: 'I will give your two sons the keys of Delhi and Lahore. They will prosper.' And prosper they did—my father as a building contractor in Delhi; and his younger brother Ujjal Singh as one of pre-Partition Punjab's biggest landowners. He later became a

Member of the Legislative Assembly and, after Independence, finance minister of Punjab and still later its governor. He ended his career as Governor of Tamil Nadu.

We Sikhs and Hindus of Hadali lived with the Muslims in an uneasy but peaceful relationship. Though we addressed their elders as uncles or aunts as they did ours, we rarely went to each other's homes except on marriages and deaths. We lived in slight awe of the Muslims because they were more numerous and much bigger built than us. Fortunately for us, they were split into different clans— Waddhals, Mastials, Awans, Janjuas, Noons and Tiwanas—and were often engaged in litigation over land, frequently murdering each other. We kept ourselves at a safe distance from them.

I recall passing their men striding down the village lanes. Most of them were over six feet tall and made as if of whipcord. They wore their well-oiled hair curling out behind their ears, stuck with small wooden or ivory combs. They normally twirled spindles with the fleece of sheep or camels to make yarn, or took their hooded falcons out for airing. Their women were also tall, slender and well proportioned. They could carry two pitchers full of water balanced on their heads, and one pitcher caught between the right arm and waist. Water splashed on their muslin shirts and ankle-length lungis, displaying the outlines of their taut, shapely, black-nippled breasts as well as their muscular, dimpled buttocks. They never looked up from the ground as they glided past, aware of men eating them up with their eyes. Though barely four years old, I became an inveterate voyeur.

Nothing very exciting happened in Hadali. Life had a soporific routine. My grandmother rose well before dawn to milk the buffaloes and put the milk in an earthen pot over smouldering embers of pats of buffalo dung. She went out into the open with neighbouring women to defecate. She pulled up a couple of buckets of water from the well and bathed herself under starlight as she mumbled the morning prayer, Japji. She spent the next half hour churning butter and buttermilk, reciting her prayers as she did so. Then she woke me up. I was allowed to defecate on the rooftop where the hot sun burnt up everything exposed to it. I washed myself. She combed my long hair and plaited it: being Sikhs we did not cut our hair. I got out my wooden takhti (slate) smeared over with yellow gaachnee (clay), my reed pen and earthen soot-inkpot. She got a bundle of stale chapatis left over from the previous evening's meal and wrapped them in her dupatta. We set out together for the Dharamsal-cum-school. Pye-dogs awaited us at our threshold. We took turns tearing up pieces of chapati and throwing them to the dogs. We kept a few in reserve for our return journey.

The Dharamsal was a short distance from our home. I was handed over to Bhai Hari Singh who was both granthi and teacher. I sat on the floor with other Hindu and Sikh boys and chanted multiplication tables in sing-song. My grandmother went to the large hall where three copies of the Granth Sahib were placed side by side on a low table. Beneath the table was an assortment of spectacles discarded by worshippers for the use of anyone they fitted. After chanting the tables, Bhai Hari Singh wrote the letters of the Gurmukhi alphabet on a board for us to copy. Though bent with age, he had a terrible temper. Any mistake he spotted on our wooden slates was rewarded with resounding kicks on our backsides. Mercifully, the lesson did not last more than an hour. My grandmother and I walked back, giving the village dogs all that remained of the chapatis. While she busied herself sweeping the floor, rolling up beds and cooking the midday meal, I went out to play hop-scotch or tip-cat (gullee-dundaa) with boys of my age.

What we did in the afternoons depended on the time of the year. Desert winters could be very cold and the days very short. There was more to do and less time to do it in. But the real winter lasted barely forty days. After a brief spring, the long summer was upon us. It became hotter day by day with temperatures rising to 125° F. We hardly ever had any rain. Our tobas (ponds) were filled with brackish rainwater coming down the Salt Range. Some of it percolated into the wells. Only a few of these wells, which were brick-and-cement lined, yielded potable water fit for human consumption. For some reason brackish wells were referred to by the male gender as khaara khoo; those which yielded sweet water were known by the diminutive, feminine gender as mitthee khooee. Most of us had pale yellow teeth with a brown line running horizontally across the upper set. This was ascribed to the impure water we drank. No matter what time of year it was, my grandmother spent her afternoons plying the charkha while mumbling Guru Arjun's *Sukhmani*—the Psalm of Peace. My memories of my grandmother are closely linked with the hum of the spinning wheel and the murmur of prayers.

The long summer months were an ordeal. The hot sands burnt the soles of one's feet. Going from one house to another we had to hug the walls to walk in their shadows, deftly avoiding blobs of shit left by children who too had found the shadows the coolest places in which to defecate. We spent most of the day indoors gossiping, or drowsily fanning away flies. It was only late in the afternoon that camels and buffaloes were taken to the tobas for watering. The buffaloes were happiest wallowing in the stagnant ponds. Boys used them as jumping boards. At sunset the cattle were driven back, the buffaloes milked and hearths lit. The entire village became fragrant with the aroma of burning camel-thorn and baking bread. Boys formed groups to go into the sand dunes to defecate. While we were at it, dung beetles gathered our turds into little marble-sized balls and rolled them to their holes in the sand. We had a unique way of cleansing ourselves. We sat on our bottoms in a line. At a given signal we raised our legs and propelled ourselves towards the winning post with our hands. By the end of the race, called gheesee, our bottoms were clean but full of sand. Later, in the night and during the early phases of the moon, we played kotla chapakee, our version of blind-man's buff. Full-moon nights on the sand dunes remain printed in my memory. We ran about chasing each other till summoned home for supper. The one threat that worked was that we might be kidnapped by dacoits. We were familiar with the names of notorious outlaws like Tora and Sultana who had spread terror in the countryside because of the number of murders and abductions they had committed.

Next to dacoits we most feared sand storms. We were used to living with dust-raising winds and spiralling dust-devils, but haneyree or jhakkhar were something else. They came with such blinding fury that there was little we could do besides crouching on the ground with our heads between our knees to prevent sand getting into our nostrils, eyes and ears. There were times when so much sand was blown that the rail track was submerged under it, and no trains ran till it was cleared. But it purged the air of flies and insects, and for the following day or two the air would be cleaner and cooler.

After the evening meal we went to our rooftops to sleep. My grandmother, who had already said her evening prayer, Rehras, recited the last prayer of the day, Kirtan Sohila. She rubbed clotted cream on my back. If her gentle ministrations did not put me to sleep, she would tell me anecdotes from the lives of our Gurus. If I were still wide awake, she would point to the stars and reprimand me: 'Don't you see what time it is? Now chup' (shut up).

The nicest time in the summer was the early morning. A cool breeze blew over the desert, picking up the fragrances of roses and jasmine that grew in our courtyards. It was the time for half sleep and fantasizing. It was all too brief. The sun came up hot, bringing with it flies and the raucous caw-cawing of crows. The blissful half hour that Urdu poets refer to as the baad-e-naseem (zephyr of early dawn) came to an end all too suddenly.

Little happened in Hadali to relieve the tedium of our daily routine. There was a murder or two every other year. But since murders were confined to the Muslims, we never got overexcited about them. Once a year there were tent-pegging competitions on the open ground near the railway station. Competitors lined up on their horses and, at a given signal, galloped towards the stakes waving their spears and yelling 'Allah Beli Ho' (Oh Allah is my best friend). After piercing the stakes they waved their spears triumphantly for all to see. They often raced passing railway trains and kept pace with them till their horses ran out of breath. I remember the first time a Sikh brought a bicycle to Hadali. He boasted that he would outrun any horse. Before a horseman could take up his challenge, we boys decided to take him on. Hadali had no metalled road and the cyclist was still wobbly on the wheels. He fared very poorly as his cycle got stuck in the sand. He became the laughing stock of the village and was thereafter mocked with the title 'Saikal Bahadur'—brave man of the bicycle.

I returned to Hadali three times after shifting to Delhi. The first time, to be initiated into reading the Granth Sahib. My elder brother, a cousin and I were made to read aloud the Japji in front of the congregation and asked to swear that we would read at least one hymn every day. None of us was able to keep our promise for very long. I went there next when practising law in Lahore. I drove to Hadali with a friend whose cousin was the manager of the salt mines. As we pulled up near the railway station, tears welled up in my eyes. I resisted the urge to go down on my knees and kiss the earth. I walked up to the Dharamsal and to the house where I was born. A man who was risaldar in the viceroy's bodyguard recognized me and spread the news to the village. By the time I left, there was a crowd to see me off.

My last visit to Hadali was in the winter of 1987. The partition of India in 1947 had brought about a complete change in its population. Not a single Sikh or Hindu remained. Our homes were occupied by Muslim refugees from Haryana. Our family haveli was divided into three equal parts, each shared by Muslim refugees from Rohtak. A new generation of Hadalians who had never seen a Sikh were then in their forties. I was uncertain of the reception they would give me. My only contact with this generation was through meeting a few young soldiers taken captive in the Indo-Pakistan War of 1971 in the prisoner-of-war camp in Dhaka. I had sought them out and written to their parents that they were safe and in good health.

I drove from Lahore and reached Hadali early in the afternoon. Village elders awaited me on the roadside with garlands of silver and gold tassels with the words Khush Amdeed—welcome—inscribed on them in Urdu. I did not recognize any of the men whose hands I shook. I was escorted to the high school ground where a dais with the Pakistan flag over it had been put up. Over 2,000 Hadalians sat in rows on chairs and on the ground. Speeches in badly pronounced, florid Urdu were delivered acclaiming me as a son of Hadali. My heart was full of gratitude. I sensed that I was about to make an ass of myself; I did. I started off well. I spoke to them in the village dialect. I said that just as they looked forward to going on pilgrimage to Mecca and Medina, coming back to Hadali at the time of the Maghreb (evening prayer) of my life was my Haj (big pilgrimage) and my Umra (small pilgrimage). And as the Prophet on his return to Mecca as victor had spent his first night wandering about the streets and praying beside the grave of his first wife, I would have liked nothing better than to be left alone to roam about the lanes of Hadali and rest my head on the threshold of the house in which I was born. Then I was overcome by emotion and broke down. They understood and forgave me. I was escorted to my former home with the entire village following me. Fireworks were let off; women standing on rooftops showered rose petals on me. Who was the author of the perfidious lie that Muslims and Sikhs were sworn enemies? No animosity had soured relations between the Muslims, Hindus and Sikhs of Hadali. Muslims had left the Sikh-Hindu Dharamsal untouched because it had been a place of worship for their departed cousins.

The Rohtak families, living in what was once our home, had done up the haveli with coloured balloons and paper buntings. The elders of the village who once knew my father had a feast laid out in my honour. There was little that I saw of Hadali that I recognized. The sand dunes which had been the playgrounds of my childhood years were gone. A canal had greened the desert. The tobas had become swamps full of reeds. The marble plaque commemorating the services of the men who had fought in World War I had been removed. I left Hadali a little before sunset, aware that I would never return to it again.

[After Khushwant Singh passed away in March 2014, a portion of his ashes was taken by train to Pakistan and buried in Hadali.—Ed]

LAST DAYS IN LAHORE

I was a lawyer practicing at the High Court of Lahore (now in Pakistan). We were a small family consisting of a wife, two children and four white leghorns—one rooster and three hens. Early in the morning, I used to let the birds out of the hatch to let them join me for my morning cup of tea. The rooster used to sit on the arm of the chair and only allowed his favourite wife to perch on my knee. I read the newspaper as best as I could amidst the clucking and the quarrelling of the birds. This continued right through the spring of the year 1947. I read of the impending transfer of power from British to Indian hands, of the Boundary Commission that was to partition India and Pakistan and of the rioting that was taking place all over Punjab. I assumed that these things would pass, that India and Pakistan would be free members of the Commonwealth and that I would stay on where I was in Lahore, whether it went to India or Pakistan, and have my morning cup of tea with my white leghorn rooster and his harem of three snow maidens. The birds gave life a sense of continuity.

Early in the August of 1947 things began to change. The riots assumed the magnitude of a massacre and it became clear that the Sikhs and Hindus would have to clear out of Pakistan. I was a Sikh, but I clung to the hope that I would be able to stay in Pakistan where I had been born and where all my closest friends, who were largely Muslim, were living.

This was not to be. One afternoon in the first week of August, I saw columns of black smoke rising from the bazaars and heard sounds of gunfire and the wailing of women.

A week before Independence, Chris Everett, head of the CID in Punjab who had studied Law with me in London, advised me to get out of Lahore. We picked up whatever we could in our hands, handed the keys of the house to a Muslim friend, Manzur Qadir, and joined the stream of Hindu and Sikh refugees going out of Pakistan into India. Escorted by six Baluch constables, my wife and I took a train to Kalka to join our two children, who had been sent ahead to their grandparents in Kasauli. We came across convoys of Muslim refugees fleeing from India into Pakistan. We heard terrible stories of murder, rape and arson. I've heard that rioters who had come to loot my house in Lahore and had been beaten off by my friend had got away with my white leghorns, which happened to be in the garden. We had no doubt of the fate that had befallen them. Then I realized that the world I had lived in and whose continuance I had taken for granted had ceased to exist.

I arrived in Delhi on 13 August 1947. The next night I was amongst the crowd outside Parliament House chanting 'Bharat Mata ki Jai'. I saw Lord Luis Mountbatten lower the Union Jack as the last viceroy of British India and hoist the Indian tricolour as the first Governor-General of free India. I heard jubilant crowds singing in the streets. I saw English officers carried aloft on shoulders by enthusiastic young men—there was an unbelievable burst of friendship towards the English. But there was an element of unreality in the celebrations because the killing and looting went on.

The only person who seemed real was Mahatma Gandhi who had refused to participate in the festivities and was going about on foot from village to village exhorting people to stop killing their neighbours. He told them that hate kills the man who hates; that Indian sages—Jain Mahavira, Gautama the Buddha, Kabir and Nanak had condemned violence as a sin and exalted non-violence as the supreme religion—Ahimsa Paramo Dharma. The grand climax came some months later when a young Hindu fanatic walked up to the Mahatma, put three bullets in his frail body and forever silenced the lone voice of sanity.

A period of remorse set in. People said that all of us were murderers of Gandhi. The killings stopped. Hindus, Muslims, and Sikhs felt ashamed of what they had done to each other. Gandhi had his greatest triumph in his martyrdom. Hadn't he said himself: 'In the midst of darkness, light exists. In the midst of untruth, truth exists.'

ON UNDERSTANDING SIKH POLITICS

Sikh politics have been in the doldrums ever since they lost their kingdom and became a part of the Indian subcontinent. For the first half a century of British rule this remained unnoticed simply because they had nothing to grouse about and much to be grateful for to their rulers. They were a miniscule minority and even in their Punjab homeland counted for no more than 13 per cent of the population of the province. Nevertheless, they were the richest landowners of Punjab paying over 40 per cent of the land revenue and water rates. A third of the British Indian Army consisted of Sikhs and a majority of the police force employed in the outposts of the Empire were also Sikhs. The situation did not call for any political skills. Sikh politics was the monopoly of Sikh princes and Zamindars. The more loyalty they expressed towards the British Crown, the better were their chances of being acknowledged as representative of the community and becoming ministers of government. The Maharaja of Patiala who was the *Farzand-i-khas* (favourite son) of the *Sarkar-e-Englishia* (English government) was the spokesman of the Sikhs. Ministers were affluent knighted landowners like Sir Vishnu Singh and later like Sir Sunder Singh Manjithia and Sir Jogendra Singh.

Sikh problems began with the introduction of democratic institutions in the country under pressure of demands for home rule. The Indian National Congress had been formed in 1885. Two years later, Sir Syed Ahmed Khan formed the United Patriotic Association exclusively for Muslims. All the Sikhs had to represent their political aspirations was the Chief Khalsa Diwan formed as late as 1902 under the leadership of Sardar (later Sir) Sunder Singh Majithia with the avowed purpose of 'cultivating loyalty to the crown'.

Punjabis were slow to respond to the demands of home rule,

which was becoming a live issue in other parts of India. Although the Indian Councils Act of 1861 authorised the setting up of provincial legislatures, Punjab did not bother to have a council till thirty-six years later. Punjabis showed the same indifference towards their district and municipal affairs. The Municipal Act was passed in 1862 and the District Boards Act in 1883 but Punjabis could not be bothered with such trifles. *The Tribune* (4 April 1883) described the few elected and nominated members as men who knew no more than to say 'Jo hukam khudawand—your lordship's orders will be obeyed.'

The Punjab Legislative Council, consisting of nine members nominated by the lieutenant governor, was established in 1897. The Sikh representation was entirely restricted to the landowning rich: Sir Khan Singh Bedi, Sir Ranbir Singh, Sir Pratap Singh, Yuvraj of Nabha, Arjan Singh Bagarian (high priest of the princely order). These worthy gentlemen distinguished themselves by observing respectful silence throughout their tenures.

The Minto-Morley Reforms of 1909 which for the first time accepted limited elections found Sikh leaders utterly unprepared for them. While Muslims got away with separate electorates and weightage, the Sikh claims for the same were ignored. Consequently, in the elections that followed not a single Sikh was elected. The governor had to oblige them by filling the Sikh quota by nominations.

The Lucknow Pact between the Congress and the Muslim League by which separate electorates and additional representation was conceded to the Muslims, took scant notice of the Sikhs. Ultimately, the Montague-Chelmsford proposals conceded the Sikh case but when they were debated along with the Lucknow Pact in the Punjab Council, an attempt by a Sikh member to insert a clause tabled for acceptance 'subject to the just claims of the Sikhs' was opposed by both Hindu and Muslim members and thrown out by six votes to two—the two being Sikhs. Every time the Sikh claim was overlooked, Sikh leaders had to plead with the government for justice. And the government came to their rescue. It was not the kind of atmosphere in which genuine political leadership could be nurtured.

WORLD WAR I

The situation began to change during World War I. By then the Ghadr Party which was dominated by the Sikh emigrants living in Canada and the United States had come to the fore as freedom fighters. The Sikh disillusionment in the War (a third of the British Indian Army that fought in Europe and Turkey were Sikhs)—the massacre at Jallianwala Bagh (being the Sikh festival, Baisakhi, the majority of victims were Sikhs) turned the Sikhs away from their traditional loyalty to the English. The Akali movement (1921–1925) completed the process. The Sikhs dispensed with the hegemony of the landed elite and threw up a middle-class leadership under the Akali Party. Virtually the last remnant of the landowning class who survived these changes was Ujjal Singh (later finance minister of Independent Punjab and Governor of Punjab and Tamil Nadu). The grass-root leaders were men like Baba Kharak Singh, Master Tara Singh, Gyani Kartar Singh or creations of the Akalis like Baldev Singh and Swaran Singh. Sikh politics came to be centred around the Shiromani Gurdwara Prabandhak Committee which became a kind of Parliament of the Sikhs. Ever since its inception in 1925 it remained under Akali control. It should be borne in mind that right from its birth the Akali party has commanded the loyalties of the vast majority of the Sikhs. Other political parties have only enjoyed marginal support—the Congress amongst urban Sikhs and the Communists in the home districts of the members of the Ghadr Party.

The two major problems that have confronted Sikh leaders over the past decades have been to find means by which they could preserve their separate identity from the parent community, the Hindus with whom they have relations of kinship, and to evolve a political identity of their own. The two problems are related and often cause confusion when students of Sikh politics try to see them separately.

Sikhism is an offshoot of Hinduism and most Sikhs are converts from Hinduism. Punjabi Hindus regard Sikhs as one of them and till recently brought up one of their sons as a Sikh, intermarried with Sikh families, worshipped in Sikh gurdwaras and recited the Gurbani which they could understand in preference to slokas from the Vedas, Upanishads or the Gita which they could not. The all-embracing character of Hinduism threatened to take Sikhism in its embrace and make the community another branch of Hindus. A Sikh who cut off his long hair and beard became a Hindu believing in Sikhism just as much as Punjabi Hindus who worshipped in Sikh gurdwaras. The dividing line between the two communities was very thin and often invisible. The resistance to absorption naturally came from the orthodox Khalsa. The scholar Kahan Singh of Nabha emphatically proclaimed 'Ham Hindu nahin hain—we are not Hindus.' It also suited the Sikhs to emphasize their not being Hindus. They had their own separate electorate, reservations in jobs and a coveted over-representation in the army. Only those Sikhs who maintained the Khalsa traditions of uncut hair and beard could avail of these privileges. British rule thus ensured the continuance of the Khalsa tradition.

PARTITION
Partition and Independence brought about cataclysmic changes in the fortunes of the Sikhs. Not only was the more prosperous half which lived in what became Pakistan uprooted and reduced to penury, but separate electorates and the special privileges they enjoyed were abolished by a stroke of the pen. Now it was the number of heads that mattered not what was in them or in the body. Sikh leaders had to devise means by which the Sikhs' separate identity could be ensured in a secular India in which they formed less than 2 per cent of the population and their prosperity restored to them. The only glimmer of hope in this otherwise bleak situation was that at least in their new homeland, East Punjab, they found themselves in a majority in certain districts. They felt that if they could carve out a state where they could be ensured of this majority continuing, they might be able to create an atmosphere where Khalsa traditions could be maintained and they could also acquire political clout. These became the motivation behind the Punjabi Suba movement which was essentially a demand for a Sikh majority state with a linguistic sugar coating. Sikh political leadership also underwent a caste and class change. It had been led by the educated, urban dwelling non-Jat Khatris and Aroras like Baba Kharak Singh and Master Tara Singh. The Partition scattered the urbanite Sikh to different cities of India and deprived it of its cohesiveness. Leadership

passed into the hands of Jats with a strong rural bias. At the grass-roots level, they were of modest education like Jathedars Gurcharan Singh Tohra, Jagdev Singh Talwandi and Sant Harchand Singh Longowal. At the state level, they were educated men like Pratap Singh Kairon, Gurnam Singh, Lachman Singh Gill and are today represented by an even more sophisticated elite consisting of men like Prakash Singh Badal and Balwant Singh—all Jats. The only exception in Jat hegemony over Sikh politics is Giani Zail Singh, a Ramgarhia. And that only because of a decline in the fortunes of the Akalis. Both the Gyani and Buta Singh, a Harijan, are creations of the Congress Party.

ANANDPUR RESOLUTION

The Anandpur Resolution passed by the Akali Party in 1973 can be understood if it is realized that it is essentially an expression of fear of absorption in the Hindu fold and a desperate attempt to reaffirm Sikh political identity. There are many versions of this resolution of which the first one drafted by the maverick Kapur Singh (dismissed from the Indian Civil Service for corruption) is couched in the most intemperate language and describes the Congress Party as a Hindu body. Even its subsequent amendments retain the seeds of separatism from the Hindus and can be construed as demanding separate nationhood for the Sikhs. Amongst its many demands is a redrawing of the boundaries of Punjab to incorporate contiguous villages now in Haryana or Himachal as well as the Ganganagar district of Rajasthan into Punjab. The pretext is that they are Punjabi-speaking, but the fact is that they are populated by Sikhs. The resolution also demands other tracts which are largely Hindu and if the demand was conceded, the Sikhs would be reduced from the 52 per cent majority they are in Punjab today to a minority. Nevertheless, the drafters of the resolution want that in this new state the voice of the Sikhs should be predominant—Khalsa ji da bol bala rahey. The Anandpur Resolution is the product of confused thinking and would need to be drastically rephrased before it can be accepted by the Sikh community at large. It is not surprising that for eight years it was left to collect dust in Akali archives and only brought out when the Akalis lost power in Punjab.

The Akalis' demands are a by-product of the Anandpur Resolution and yet another attempt to affirm their religious and political identity. They have themselves obviated any chances of their returning to power by alienating Punjabi Hindus from them. Some of their basic demands like the declaration of Chandigarh as Punjab's exclusive capital (without bartering away of Fazilka and Abohar), a fairer distribution of river waters, control over dams and hydroelectric works, setting up of industries are without doubt just and will have to be conceded by the central government in the course of time. But if the Akalis had carried Punjabi Hindus with them, their task would have been much easier.

The rise of fundamentalism spearheaded by Jarnail Singh Bhindranwale can likewise be understood as the last-ditch battle to preserve the separate identity of the Khalsa Panth. The militant Dal Khalsa, the Keertan Jathas and the Khalistanis are a by-product of the same sense of insecurity: if we don't have a state of our own we will be sunk in the ocean of Hinduism.

Can this volatile situation be defused? I have not the slightest doubt that it can be, provided the government means business and does not deliberately prolong the confrontation to gain political leverage in the northern states. The Akalis' legitimate demands, which now have the support of Punjabi Hindus, must be conceded forthwith and with good grace. It will strengthen the hands of Akali moderates and isolate the extremists like Talwandi, Sukhjinder Singh and Bhindranwale. Moderate Akalis' must also reciprocate by renouncing once and for all, talk of separate nationhood: we are a separate religious community but belong to the Indian nation. Separate nationhood has sinister implications and will be suicidal for the Sikhs—20 per cent of us live outside Punjab and our future will be put in jeopardy. It is now for the government to break the impasse. If it does not do so in the near future, it runs the risk of alienating the sympathies of the entire Sikh community.

On 22 February 1984, Sumeet Singh was murdered. Details that I learned from members of the bereaved family had a bearing on the tragedy that was then being enacted almost daily in Punjab and Haryana. Sumeet was one of the four sons of Navtej Singh whose father, Gurbaksh Singh, had set up a commune of like-minded liberals called Preetnagar between Lahore and Amritsar. He also edited the most widely-read Punjabi monthly magazine, *Preetlari*. After the partition of Punjab in 1947, Preetnagar became a border town on the Indian side. After Gurbaksh Singh's death, Navtej took over the affairs of the commune as well as the editorship of *Preetlari*. And when Navtej died two years ago, Sumeet took over these responsibilities.

Like many Punjabis, this Preetnagar family was not conscious of differences between Hindus and Sikhs. Some wore long hair and beards; others did not. Sumeet had cut his hair, his brothers were Keshadharis. Sumeet married Poonam, the daughter of the well-known trade union leader Madan Lal Didi.

A week before his murder, Sumeet, who was in Delhi, boarded a Punjab Roadways bus for Chandigarh. Near Panipat, the bus was surrounded by a Hindu mob. Since Sumeet wore a steel kara, he was hauled out to explain his identity. He told them he was a Hindu. The leaders of the mob were not satisfied and wanted to beat him up. It was the Hindu bus driver who braved the mob and threatened to fight anyone who dared to touch Sumeet. The sacred kara almost cost Sumeet his life. It was a Hindu who saved it.

A week later, Sumeet and his youngest brother, Ratnikant Singh, who is Keshadhari, decided to go to Amritsar on their scooter to do some shopping. At Lopoki they ran into an ambush by four Sikh gunmen out on a killing spree. They had already shot a couple of

Hindus when they came upon the two brothers and yelled, 'Ik aur shikaar mil gaya (We've found another prey)', obviously referring to the short-haired Sumeet. Ratnikant swore that Sumeet was his brother. He took off his turban and put it on Sumeet's head to show how alike they looked. Sumeet held up his kara to show he was a Sikh. Nothing worked. The thugs shot him in the head and shoulder and left him for dead. The shots did not kill Sumeet. As he crumpled to the ground, the scooter fell on him. Ratnikant advised his brother to feign death till he got help. The killers went about their bloody mission. Before running away from Lopoki, they had another look at Sumeet, and seeing that he was still alive, pumped three more rounds into him. Thus these so-called Sikhs took the life of a fellow-Sikh either believing him to be a Hindu or a Sikh whose views were unpalatable to them.

The killing of Sumeet caused enormous revulsion amongst Punjabis against killer squads and their arch-patron, Bhindranwale. At Sumeet's funeral, amongst those who denounced these villains was Bibi Rajinder Kaur, Akali MP and daughter of the late Master Tara Singh. For a change, she recalled her Hindu ancestry (Masterji was a Malhotra Hindu till the age of eleven) and named several Akali leaders whose grandparents were Hindus. An eminent Akali leader who came wearing a white turban instead of the Akali steel-blue stated openly that for once he felt ashamed of wearing the badge of his party. As the Gandhi cap, once honoured as the symbol of rectitude, has today become a symbol of corruption, so the once respected steel-blue of the Akalis was becoming the symbol of all that was venal.

There was a time when the militant Khalsa had found his mission in the words repeated at the end of every prayer: neotian di oat (saviour of the helpless), ne aasrian da aasra (hope of those who have lost all hope), nithavaan di thaan (refuge for the homeless) and nipattian di patt (honour of those dishonoured). All this was being bartered away by a handful of blue-turbaned men to attain their selfish ends. It was significant that the last article Sumeet wrote in *Preetlari* was titled 'Nahin taan bahut der ho chukee hovegee' (Otherwise it will have become too late).

Things had come to such a pass that only the naive could have cherished the illusion that the clouds would soon lift, rainbows span the heavens and skylarks sing songs of peace over the golden wheatlands of Punjab. And only fools would have believed that wounds inflicted by the people on the people with the tacit approval of their foolishly short-sighted leaders could be healed, that Punjabi Hindus and Sikhs would once again be falling into each other's arms, worshipping in each other's temples and giving their sons and daughters in marriage to each other. All that was buried in the past. The damage that had been inflicted was irreparable. The perpetrators of Punjab's tragedy would get away with their crimes with only the pages of history to record their vile deeds and the ineptitude of the government.

The lapses were manifold. So were the doubts in my mind. Would criminals who spilt innocent blood be brought to trial and punished? Would people who saw them commit these crimes now be bold enough to testify against them? I doubted it. Peace bought at the price of condoning crime is always an uneasy and fragile one.

Would anyone dare to ask Akali leaders by what convolution of logic did they maintain that burning a part of the Constitution (as they did on 27 February 1984) that they had sworn to uphold in the name of God, did not amount to disrespect for it? What faith could people place on their word of honour? What guarantee was there that they would not raise new issues as they had done after the forty-five demands regarding a separate personal law for the Sikhs and the amendment of Article 25? Would they actively aid the administration in nabbing criminals? Would they abjure forever talk of separate nationhood and amend the Anandpur Sahib Resolution? I doubted it. A peace bought without clarifying fundamental points of difference is a truce that may be violated by anyone at any time.

The government, on its part, deserved little credit for the way it had handled the Punjab crisis. Like the British, successive governments of free India had continued to treat it as a producer of grain and human gun fodder. On the plea that it was a border state, few industries were allowed to be set up there. Once yield from land had reached its optimum with the Green Revolution, decline set in. And with decline, disenchantment, restlessness and discord. It took Mr M. A. Jinnah and the Muslim League almost a decade to nurture the cactus of separation on a fertile soil; it took the government and the Akalis less than three years' tillage in the most barren land to sprout the thickets of Hindu-Sikh separatism. The real job of giving Punjab more industries and finishing river projects planned many years ago to give the state and its neighbours more water and hydroelectric power fell by the wayside. The government went on talking. The people went on listening without believing a word of it.

What followed is now common knowledge. It was Bhindranwale's guns that began to do the actual talking. The Akali leaders were cowed by fear into making inane statements and did not criticize him for the hateful pronouncements he was making or have the courage to tell him that a place of worship should not be used as a sanctuary for criminals or be converted into a fortress. On its part, the administration was paralysed and, in full view of hundreds of armed policemen, arms continued to be smuggled into the Golden Temple complex.

Despite continued terrorist activity over months until the end of May 1984, the government evidently did not think that storming the Golden Temple and flushing out Bhindranwale and his supporters would put an end to the violence in the state. It was the Akalis' decision to step up their agitation by blocking the movement of food grains and the possibility of increased terrorist activity that compelled the government to come to the conclusion that enough was enough. It undoubtedly felt that a major surgical operation of the dimension carried out was necessary to prevent the cancer of violence from spreading further.

But what took place on 6 June was in fact a forcible entry made with the help of guns and tanks, resulting in a bloodbath the like of which has not been witnessed in the Golden Temple since it was built more than 380 years ago. It was an ironic coincidence of history that the tragic episode should have taken place following the anniversary homage to Arjun Dev, the builder of the Harmandir, compiler of the Sikh sacred scripture, the Granth Sahib, the first martyr of the Sikhs and the man who gave the temple and the city in which it stands, the name Amritsar—a pool of nectar.

It is unlikely that we will ever get to know the truth about how the invasion was planned and executed, the number of people killed and the damage done to the temple. Government and Akali versions are and will forever be at variance. However, there can be little doubt that government handouts on the subject lack credibility. And in slaying Jarnail Singh Bhindranwale the government has, in effect, invested the mad monk of yestermonths with the halo of martyrdom he scarcely deserves. Far from crushing the Khalistan movement, it has given it the sustenance it lacked and weakened the hands of Sikhs like me who are bitterly opposed to it.

It is tempting to compare the two massacres in the history of Amritsar. The first took place sixty-five years ago in neighbouring Jallianwala Bagh on 13 April 1919. It was on Baisakhi, the day Guru Gobind Singh founded the Khalsa Panth. The figure of casualties put out by the Punjab government after the Jallianwala Bagh massacre was challenged by the committee formed by the Indian National Congress, which maintained that the death toll was more than double of what was put out by the government. Most historians believe that the final toll was 379 dead and over 2,000 wounded.

In the second episode, the government of the day conceded that over 300 were killed. The Akalis put the figure at well over 1,000, including women and children. The one important difference between the two events is that while General Dyer ordered his Gurkha platoon to open fire on an entirely unarmed and peaceful assembly, General Ranjit Singh Dyal (whose namesake rebuilt the Harmandir in marble and gold leaf) had his men storm the temple complex that had been converted into a fortress and defended by desperados armed with sophisticated weapons. The one important sequel that the two episodes may have is that while the Jallianwala Bagh massacre became the turning point in the history of India's freedom movement, the massacre in the Harmandir may well become a similar turning point in the history of the Khalistan movement.

The vast majority of Indians felt that the government had allowed matters to go from bad to worse and welcomed the decision to grasp the Bhindranwale nettle with an iron hand. If government spokesmen are to be believed, the action had created a sense of relief amongst the general public. All the major political parties and newspapers of the country also approved of the action. The only exception to the otherwise national approval were the Sikhs. The Akalis understandably condemned this action. And no self-respecting Sikh had a kind word to say for the government or the Sikh general it deployed to carry out the operation. The number of innocent people slain increased the desecration of the Parikrama and the Akal Takht was permanently bruised in the brutal memory of the Khalsa Panth.

It was this loss that every one of the world's 14 million Sikhs mourned, and not the deaths of Bhindranwale and his gunmen who met the fate they had asked for. Sikhs expected their countrymen to share their grief. Instead, most Indians rejoiced and toasted each other over the military action.

When I surrendered the Padma Bhushan awarded to me in protest, many journalists were very critical of me. I was asked whether I felt anything when Atwal, Harbans Singh Manchanda, Tiwari, Jagat Narain, Romesh Chandra and Pratap Singh were murdered. I was asked what I had to say when innocent Hindus were picked out at random from buses and slain and banks looted. My answer was that I felt these killings deeply for, amongst other reasons, Jagat Narain, Romesh Chandra and Tiwari were my friends. What is more, I condemned the perpetrators of these dastardly crimes in more forthright language than any other Indian journalist. Did any of them dare to describe Bhindranwale as demented? I did, in print, and in many broadcasts over the BBC. Did any journalist use such words to condemn Bhindranwale when he was alive? No. Only I did and came to be a marked man on Bhindranwale's list.

I was asked if I tried to influence my friends in the Akali Dal to stop their hoodlums from doing what they were doing. My answer was that I never had any friends in the Akali Dal and to the best of my knowledge none of the hoodlums belonged to the Akali Dal but to terrorist organizations which sprang up in the wake of killings in faked encounters by Darbara Singh's police. Although I had no friends amongst the Akalis, I castigated their leaders in no uncertain terms for allowing Bhindranwale to entrench himself in the temple complex, desecrate the temple by his presence and hateful declamations he made from the Akal Takht. Admittedly, I did not go to the temple to offer satyagraha. I am not that kind of journalist.

In Karnal, Panipat and Yamunanagar scores of gurdwaras and Sikh properties were looted and burnt. Incidents of Sikhs being harassed and manhandled continued. While cars driven by non-Sikhs were allowed to pass checkposts, those which had Sikh passengers were halted and searched. Amongst those who were subjected to this kind of humiliating discrimination of whom I have personal knowledge was Bibi Amarjit Kaur, member, Rajya Sabha and her husband, a Sikh colonel and an air force officer, both in uniform. In some cases, police officers acting in this high-handed manner were suspended. But this was only when Sikhs so maltreated were important enough to lodge complaints with people who mattered. Others suffered the indignity and chewed the cud of bitterness.

Most people unquestionably accepted the government's contention that it had no option but to send the army in and blast Bhindranwale out of the Akal Takht. I am no military expert and yet I maintained (as I did in Parliament) that commandos in plain clothes and even a military action limited to occupying the Guru ka Langar, depriving Bhindranwale's men of food and fuel and forcing them out would have been a much less bloody affair, saved hundreds of innocent lives and the extensive damage to sacred precincts.

The reason why I was so upset by the army action is that it created fertile soil for sowing the seeds of Khalistan and made the task of Sikhs who, like me, were opposed to it, much more difficult. As far as I am personally concerned, let me reiterate, I never have, nor ever will compromise with any move to dismember my Motherland. Khalistan will be made over my dead body.

1984: A DARK YEAR

JANUARY

For many years I ushered in the New Year drinking champagne and embracing women I scarcely knew. Most of the following morning was spent nursing a hangover and resolving never to touch liquor again. After middle age overtook me I made no distinction between New Year's Eve and other nights. While others were drinking, dancing, singing and popping balloons, I would go off to sleep and the New Year would steal over me as I snored. I would rise at 4.30 a.m., switch on the BBC and listen to the news. This year was no different. The telephone rang. It was a call from Bombay, a voice from the distant past I could barely recognize wished me a happy New Year. It was like 'breeding lilacs out of the dead land, mixing / Memory and desire, stirring / Dull roots with spring rain'. Daylight broke through the mist. It was cold. The tops of the trees caught the orange of the morning sun and the dew-drenched lawn sparked in the sunlight. A woodpecker alighted on the siris tree and crackled 'noo-noo-year, noo-noo-year'. At breakfast, the widow of a cousin who had died on New Year's Eve the previous year came to reminisce about her husband. On the birth of a new year we talked of death. In the afternoon Shahidul Haq and Himayatuddin of Bangladesh dropped in. Himayat's wife was expecting their second child. 'We hoped she (they already have a son) would be born on New Year's Day,' said Himayat's wife. For a change, on the birth of the New Year we talked of a new life to come. The next visitor was my latest heartthrob, a lovely girl saddened by her experience of life. She unburdened her heart which she has never given to anyone yet. But a fellow who pursued her with flattery, gifts and proposals of marriage turned out to be a philanderer. She was relieved she discovered the truth about him in the nick of time, but she was sad that the year should begin with betrayal. I acquired my new Maruti. It is a lovely little car which taxi drivers contemptuously describe as sabun-daani, a soap dish. I took K. K. Birla for a joyride and told him it was half the price and twice as good as the Birla product, the Ambassador.

The following week I ran into Jacqueline Kennedy and her son John. We had an hour together in the VIP lounge at Palam. She looked her years and was somewhat incoherent in her speech. I could not believe a woman like her could have sold herself to an obnoxious character like Aristotle Onassis for his billions; nor that her handsome son could, after the assassinations of his father and uncle, want to become a politician. I had John over for dinner and asked him who he would like to meet, politicians or pretty girls? Without hesitation he replied, 'Politicians.' However, I asked both. He ignored the girls and spoke only to politicians.

This was followed by an evening with Namita and Rajiv Gokhale. Her novel *Paro* will be published in London. She was bubbling with excitement. Then presided over a poetry reading by the policeman-poet, Keki Daruwalla. Two lines struck me as prophetic:

During the big drought which is surely going to come
the doves will look up for clouds, and it will rain hawks.

It continued to be very cold. But the chill winds did not dampen the enthusiasm of our birds, woodpeckers still cluster about the siris. Every morning painted storks wheel in the blue skies, flying and heading for the Yamuna.

How is it I overlooked the most important day in January? The Gantantra Diwas on the 26th? Because over the years my enthusiasm for celebrating anything has been diminishing. Shame on me.

FEBRUARY
Despite the severe cold, the cherry tree has blossomed. If the cherry flowers are here can spring be far behind? Asha and Vasanth Seth (Great Eastern Shipping) dropped in. He says Bombay has become so congested that the only way he can get fresh air is by sleeping in

his yacht anchored offshore. His holidays are spent sailing amongst the creeks. If every Bombay man owned a yacht, we could walk over the sea to Karachi.

I have two birthdays—one official and the other nearer the real date of nativity. I do not celebrate either of them. But there are friends who never fail to wish me on 2 February. Inder Malhotra of the *Times of India* is a born birthday greeter. So are the Advanis who lived in the apartment above mine in Colaba. Jyoti never forgets to send me a telegram. This year there was nothing much to celebrate. Bhindranwale was causing me acute anguish. I wrote a profile of the 'sant' for Hyderabad's *Newstime* describing him as a 'mad monk'. One of these days his goons will get me. Little did he know that he would not be around on my next fake birthday.

A heavy mist spread over the city on the morning of the 4th and brought air services to a standstill. My flight to Islamabad to attend a journalists' meet organized by *The Muslim* was delayed by two hours; I missed the connecting flight at Lahore and had to spend the night and next day in the city which had been my home till Partition and where many of my dearest friends are buried. I rang them up (the living) and next morning had a lobby full of my Pakistani brothers, their wives and children. They were worried over India's aggressive postures. The latest case was the disappearance of two servants of an Indian diplomat from Islamabad. Our embassy protested against their abduction. The protest boomeranged as a few days later both men surfaced in India (nobody knows how they got across the border).

Three days in Pakistan listening to speeches from their foreign minister, I & B minister and retired generals protesting their goodwill towards India was assuring. More than India they were worried by the Russian presence in Afghanistan.

I returned home to a Punjab coming to the boil. Punjab bandh was total. It was followed by Hindu-Sikh riots in Punjab and a massive Hindu backlash in Karnal, Panipat and Yamunanagar, resulting in considerable loss of Sikh lives and property. At the Golden Temple there was an exchange of fire between Bhindranwale's men and the armed police. When will Akali leaders and Bhindranwale's gunmen realize that for what they do in Punjab, the price is paid by Sikhs living in other parts of India? In India life is cheap. What are half a dozen men stabbed to death when a few rail bogeys off the track can take a toll of over forty lives as one did near Ballabhgarh?

I spent three days with President Zail Singh. I flew with him in his plane to Poona. He proceeded by helicopter to Rajkot to garland the statue of Shivaji. On board were his daughter and her husband, also the grandson who had earned his displeasure for shooting pigeons in Rashtrapati Bhavan. None of the family could have known that the angel of death hovered over some members of his family.

I rejoined him in Bombay. All next morning I was on his yacht while he took the salute from ships and submarines of the Indian navy lined off the sea from the Gateway of India. The naval review was a boring affair—ship after ship with its crew lined on the deck, doffing their caps and yelling 'Rashtrapati ji ki Jai'. I caught glimpses of Indira Gandhi, Rajiv and Sonia who were on the yacht following ours. Throughout the two hours that the ordeal lasted I could see Indira Gandhi going up and down the deck, tireless as ever.

When I got back home to Delhi it had turned cold again. The sky was overcast and it started to drizzle. However, the weather did not dampen the spirits of parliamentarians who reassembled on the 23rd. Affairs of Punjab should have been given top priority; the president scarcely mentioned them in his address to the two houses.

Salman Rushdie came to India on the invitation of *Gentleman* magazine. After addressing a select audience at the India International Centre, he and Anita Desai, who was amongst the last six novelists under consideration for the Booker Prize, dropped in for a drink. The next evening (27th) Salman addressed a large gathering on politics and the novel—he blew to smithereens pretensions of the Raj novelists like Paul Scott, Kayo, and even E. M. Forster for not really knowing India or Indians.

MARCH

At a lunch given by Murli Deora at the Taj in Bombay, I was told of Prabha Dutt's death in Delhi. I slipped out of the party to return to my room to shed tears of tribute to my grey-eyed young colleague whom I had admired, respected and loved. It was a sad homecoming—first to call on Prabha's husband, 'Speedy' Dutt, and a few days later to hear of the passing of another friend, I. S. Johar (11th), in Bombay and writing to his re-united ex-wife Rama Bans.

March is in some ways one of our two 'autumns'. Neem, peepul and mahua shed their leaves to don new ones for the summer. The days began to lengthen and spring slowly turns to summer with the koel's full-throated cry and the barbets incessant calling to each other.

March is named after Mars, the god of war. Very appropriately, the Soviets promised massive military aid to help us preserve our freedom against foreign intervention. Meanwhile, we had plenty of violence within the country. There were fisticuffs in the Bengal Assembly (19th); a third attempt was made on the life of Darbara Singh, chief minister of Punjab (17th) and on the 19th H. S. Manchanda was murdered in broad daylight by Sikh terrorists. It was ironic as Manchanda was the only Sikh member of a Hindu family.

The Rajya Sabha shed a third of its members to make way for a new batch. This time most of them were picked by Rajiv Gandhi— hence Suresh Kalmadi's pejorative for the Upper House as 'Rajiv Sabha'. But there were a few notable entrants: the industrialist K. K. Birla (Independent), the newspaperman Desh Bandhu Gupta (Congress I) and the breathtakingly lovely film star Jayalalithaa (AIADMK).

Some literary asides deserve mention. Amongst my visitors was Kenneth Rose, biographer of King George V and Lord Curzon—he came to track down the family of the Munshi of Agra who taught Urdu to Queen Victoria. Gillian Tindall, author of a book on Bombay, gave a talk on places of literature. I played the role of an 'extra' in a film on Amrita Pritam. Historian Dr Ganda Singh and editor Sadhu Singh Hamdard were amongst those awarded the Padma Bhushan. The social worker Bhagat Puran Singh, the 'bearded Mother Teresa of Punjab', got a Padma Shri. All three men were to return these honours three months later.

Not very surprising that the Holi festival (17th) was a dull affair. It was too chilly to dowse people with coloured water and there was not the usual goodwill between the communities to take liberties with each other.

APRIL

It was indeed a cruel month. The hatred simmering in Punjab exploded into violence. Amongst those who were killed were Harbans Lal Khanna, BJP member of Punjab assembly, and Dr V. N. Tiwari (MP) who had replaced Nargis Dutt in the seat next to mine in the Rajya Sabha. Also a number of Nirankaris including women and children. The terrorists did not spare each other.

To prove that the government's stern measures after taking over the administration had not affected them, the terrorists set fire to thirty-seven railway stations at about the same time of the night (15th).

I made my little contribution to the debate on Punjab and was perhaps the only one to condemn Bhindranwale and the Akalis, and warn the government of the perils of dilatory politics in dealing with incendiary material. The home minister P. C. Sethi scarcely listened to what I or anyone else had to say.

Voices from the past came in the shape of ex-ambassador Ellsworth Bunker and his wife, Carol Laise. He is in his nineties; she almost thirty years younger. Both have innumerable Indian friends and visit India every year. This was Ellsworth's last visit to Delhi; he died a few months later.

By mid-April we were in mid-summer. The siris which had perfumed the breezes of spring shed its pom-poms; neem flowers were strewn on tarmac roads like layers of sawdust. Agitated lapwings tossed about by hot, squally winds were deliriously demanding 'did-ye did-ye do it? did-ye-do it?' The elite have been swarming to bathing pools; in the evenings, anti-mosquito squads pump anti-mosquito smoke over the city; at night, the hum of mosquitoes is louder than the roar of traffic.

The winter that we experienced this year was colder than past winters; the summer warmer than most summers, with temperatures soaring into the mid-forties and staying there for many days and nights. Even the seasonal dust storms followed by hail did not cool the hellfires. This year there were not as many electricity breakdowns but many taps ran dry when the need to slake thirst and wash sweat away were the acutest.

Vir Sanghvi and Malavika Rajbans came to interview me for

Imprint. Their piece would be the instrument of my final breach with Maneka Gandhi and her mother.

Summer brings many aches and pains. One evening of indiscreet drinking gave me gout. At Bharat Ram's party on the birth anniversary of his father, Sir Shri Ram (founder of the DCM empire), I ran into a childhood friend, Lala Pratap Singh. Because of arthritis of the knee, he could barely walk. On the other hand his wife, Savitri (daughter of Shri Ram's brother Sir Shankar Lal), had overcome cancer which had only a couple of years ago been declared incurable.

Events in Punjab were fast moving towards a denouement. My friend, Ramesh Chandra, son of Lala Jagat Narain, was gunned down. Hindu-Sikh riots followed taking a toll of twenty-eight lives in one day. Not to be outdone, in Maharashtra, organized and well-prepared Hindu mobs carried death and destruction, killing upwards of three hundred poor, defenceless Muslim weavers of Bhiwandi. The jayanti of Gautama the Buddha fell on the 15th, and went by with the usual homilies about his message of tolerance amongst humans.

Sikhs are slowly but surely losing their status as the pampered elite of India. An instance of the growing animus against the community was an article published in the *Sunday Observer* (29 April) which was the subject of a 'Special Mention' in the Rajya Sabha. It was written by one Vatsayana on the Rashtrapati's visit to the Asiatic Society in Calcutta. It made fun of him dyeing his beard with shoe polish, his ignorance of Darwin, the Earth being round and his proclivity for female flesh. This was editor Vinod Mehta's idea of humour. The leader of the House took note of it and when the matter came up before the Press Council the editor was reprimanded.

Mrs Gandhi's quarrel with her daughter-in-law Maneka was extended to include custody of Sanjay and Maneka's child, Feroze Varun Gandhi. Mrs Sunanda Bhandare, wife of Congress MP Murli Bhandare, served notice on Maneka, questioning the way the child was being exploited by her for political purposes. Maneka countered it with similar charges against Mrs Gandhi. Mrs Bhandare was later elevated to the bench of the Delhi High Court.

India was becoming too hot for me. I took off to Libya where I spent a liquor-free week listening to praises of Colonel Gaddafi's *Green*

Book. Mrs Gandhi had been in Tripoli a couple of weeks earlier and had received a great welcome. The city was still plastered with her pictures. A few days after her visit an attempt was made on Colonel Gaddafi's life and reportedly over three hundred Libyans were killed in the shootout. Libya is an uneasy country trying to bridge a gap of centuries within a few years.

JUNE

June 1984 will go down as the most fateful month in the history of independent India. The Indian Army moved most of its units into Punjab. On the 3rd, in an exchange of fire at the Golden Temple, eleven people were killed. Akali leaders, as reckless as ever, decided to impede movements of grain outside the state. The final die was cast. The army surrounded Amritsar and cut it off from the country when thousands of pilgrims were there to commemorate the martyrdom anniversary of the founder of the temple, Guru Arjun. A sporadic exchange of fire began between army units and Bhindranwale's men entrenched in the Akal Takht, the parikrama, and three towers that overlooked the temple complex. Curfew was imposed on the city, journalists expelled and strict censorship imposed on news. Whatever we know of the events that followed is what the government decided we ought to know or from unverified versions of those who were witnesses to the ghastly tragedy that followed. However, all are agreed that although the army gave many opportunities to the pilgrims to get out, not many heeded the warning—either because of the erratic imposition of curfew or indecisiveness. After knocking off the snipers atop the towers on the 5th, the army stormed into the temple to be met with withering fire from Bhindranwale's men. Tanks were brought in. They smashed their way into the parikrama and blasted the Akal Takht, killing Bhindranwale and most of his closest associates including General (retd) Shabeg Singh and Amrik Singh. Sporadic firing continued for another three days. How many people died? According to the government's White Paper, 92 army personnel and about 543 civilians. The Akali version put the figure of civilian casualties at over five thousand, a large proportion being pilgrims including women and children. Rajiv Gandhi later admitted that over seven hundred army personnel had died in 'Operation Blue Star'. The action created widespread resentment amongst the Sikhs. Over two thousand soldiers defected from their centres; some were shot, others arrested. Two Sikh MPs, several MLAs and civil servants resigned; many surrendered honours conferred on them.

On 8 June, President Zail Singh and on 23 June, Mrs Gandhi visited the temple and saw the damage done with their own eyes.

For weeks following 'Operation Blue Star' the army combed Sikh temples and villages in pursuit of extremists. To this day no one knows the extent of the loss of life and property entailed by this exercise.

On 10 June we had our first pre-monsoon shower; this was a day before I saw the monsoon bird (*Clamator jacobinus*). On the afternoon of 14 June, Maneka stormed into my study, flung a copy of *Imprint* at my face and stormed out of the house. This was followed a week later by a two-page typed letter from her mother, Amtesh Anand; it was delivered by a lawyer who made me sign a receipt. I read only the first para and then put it away amongst my books. I expected some reaction but not as exaggerated as the one I got. They were not my kind of people—they are self-centred and unconcerned with what happens to other people. I was relieved that the association was at an end.

There was a heavy downpour on the 19th followed by rainless days and the return of dust storms. What a month.

JULY

Having done with Punjab, the government turned to neighbouring Kashmir. On the night when all Muslims, including Chief Minister Dr Farooq Abdullah, were celebrating Id, his brother-in-law, G. M. Shah, manipulated the defection of a sizeable number of Dr Abdullah's followers and presented them before an amenable governor, Jagmohan. Farooq Abdullah's ministry was promptly dismissed and replaced by Shah and his turncoats. This was Mrs Gandhi's eidee (Id gift) to Farooq, one-time family friend. Violence erupted in the valley.

Meanwhile, Sikh terrorists continued to demonstrate that they had not been overcome. On the 3rd, they hijacked an Air India plane with 240 passengers abroad and took it to Pakistan. The Pakistan government returned the plane with its crew and passengers but detained the hijackers.

The monsoon continued to be erratic. It rained on the 13th and 14th. I took myself to Amritsar to see the damage done and interview people who had witnessed 'Operation Blue Star'. The city bristled with soldiers, the citizens were resentful, sullen and scared. Contrary to the government's contention that no damage had been done to the Harmandir Sahib, I counted scores of fresh bullet marks on its walls. And, contrary to claims of having preserved the sanctity of the shrine, I saw a notice alongside the Akal Takht saying 'No smoking or drinking allowed here'.

The army had overlooked taking it off when it allowed pilgrims to re-enter. I cited this evidence in my speech on the White Paper in Rajya Sabha (25th) and was jeered by the treasury benches.

Rain or no rain, on the 28th there were more monsoon birds to be seen in gardens and parks than before.

AUGUST

Warm, sultry, drizzly. Punjab was not the only troubled state. Tamil resentment against the treatment meted out to their kinsmen by the Sri Lankan government found expression in the exploding of a bomb (the third such explosion) at Madras International Airport killing thirty-two people. I saw some of the debris when I went to the city at the invitation of the Rashtriya Swayamsevak Sangh (RSS). It seems the only Hindus willing to take a sympathetic view of the plight of the Sikhs and eager to reclaim them as brethren belong to right-wing political and social groups. Meanwhile, government stooges continued their activities in Punjab. To counteract the high priests' verdict of 'guilty' pronounced against Santa Singh Nihang, who flouted Sikh sentiment by undertaking to rebuild the Akal Takht, and Minister Buta Singh who put him up to it, the two organized a Sarbat Khalsa meet in Amritsar to revoke the hukumnamah issued against them. It was an entirely Congress (I) sponsored show. The Akali response to it was to call a world Sikh meet which, though declared illegal, was a much bigger affair.

The government continued its aggressive postures. After ridding itself of a recalcitrant chief minister in Sikkim, subverting Farooq Abdullah's government in Kashmir, it suborned the loyalties of N. T. Rama Rao's followers in Andhra Pradesh. Governor Ram Lal, earlier removed as chief minister of Himachal Pradesh on charges of corruption in his family, dismissed Rama Rao's government and installed turncoat Bhaskar Rao in his place. Rama Rao, who had just got back from the US after heart surgery, mustered his followers and demonstrated before President Zail Singh in Delhi that he still commanded a majority in the Andhra Pradesh Assembly. The Opposition parties rallied around N. T. Rama Rao in a massive demonstration of support. Ram Lal was compelled to resign, but Bhaskar Rao was given time to win over more MLAs. Prices ranged from between five to twenty lakhs per defecting MLA.

On the 22nd, Venkataraman was elected vice president. On the 24th, the Rajya Sabha bid farewell to Hidayatullah. The next day Punjab was again in the news with yet another IAF plane hijacked by Sikh extremists to Lahore. Once more Pakistan returned the plane and passengers—this time the hijackers as well.

The monsoon which had been eccentric made up for its sluggishness with four days of heavy showers at the end of the month.

SEPTEMBER

The month started off with heavy rain; better late than never. And the Opposition maintained heavy pressure on the Congress (I) to test its strength in the AP Assembly. Bhaskar Rao's crude attempts to buy support came to naught and on the 15th, N. T. Rama Rao was re-crowned chief minister of Andhra Pradesh amidst scenes of jubilation. The Congress (I)'s clumsier attempts to foment communal trouble and use it as an excuse to impose President's Rule resulted in extensive damage to Muslim property and life in Hyderabad.

Punjab affairs seemed to be on the boil. On the 27th, I was in Chandigarh and met Governor Satarawala. I impressed on him the need for more industry in the state to absorb educated young men who would otherwise turn to violence. He made a note of what I said. Three days later the keys of the treasury (toshakhana) were handed over to the head priests and after four months of occupation the army was withdrawn from the Golden Temple complex. Unfortunately, this was done under threat of a massive morcha of Sikhs to liberate the temple; hence the gesture lost the element of magnanimity and touch of healing.

OCTOBER
It is a bad month for assassinations. Not many Octobers ago, North Koreans succeeded in killing seventeen South Koreans including four cabinet ministers in Rangoon. Earlier this month the IRA exploded a bomb in a Brighton hotel which narrowly missed killing Margaret Thatcher, prime minister of England. Our own prime minister was not so lucky. Her two Sikh assassins took no chances, shooting her at close range and pumping over a dozen bullets into her frail body. As if it was not bad enough for men of honour bound to protect her betraying the trust reposed in them, there were Sikhs in the US, England and even in India who were foolish enough to celebrate the murder and invited, within minutes of her death being confirmed, the wrath of the majority community on the heads of the entire community. This bloodbath washed out the goodwill created by the participation of a sizeable number of Hindus in the kar seva of the Harmandir.

NOVEMBER
Anti-Sikh riots broke out in many parts of India, taking a heavy toll of Sikh life and property. Although government spokesmen put the figure of the Sikh dead at a little over a thousand, non-official estimates put it at over six thousand, half of it in Delhi. Equally savage was violence in Kanpur, Calcutta and Bihar. Hundreds of gurdwaras and thousands of Sikh homes, taxis and trucks were burnt. The pattern of violence indicated organized, well-planned action. In most places the mobs were led by members of the Congress Party. Hindus, where they could, helped their Sikh neighbours against arsonists and looters who largely came from surrounding villages and jhuggi-jhonpri colonies. Hindu right-wing groups, notably the RSS and BJP, rendered service to their afflicted Sikh brethren. Over fifty thousand Sikhs were rendered homeless.

The administration finally woke up to its responsibility after the orgy of killing, arson and loot had gone unchecked by the police for three days and nights. The lieutenant governor of Delhi was sacked (but oddly enough replaced by the home secretary who should have owned some of the responsibility for earlier inactivity); the police commissioner and many of the prime minister's security personnel were suspended or transferred. The home minister is yet to explain his own paralysis in the face of crisis. The one man who rose to supreme heights in the crisis was Rajiv Gandhi. He made a most dignified statement on his mother's assassination and as soon as her body had been cremated (over a hundred heads of states were present at her funeral), he spent the entire night visiting affected areas and ordering the army to put down violence with an iron hand. If he had only done this two days earlier, the story of the Sikhs would have been different.

[This piece is an edited version of Khushwant Singh's unpublished journal of 1984. There are no entries for May and December—Ed]

A RIOT OF PASSAGE

There are two anniversaries so deeply etched in my mind that every year they come around, I recollect with pain what happened on those two days. One is 31 October, when Mrs Gandhi was gunned down by her two Sikh security guards. The other is the following day, when the 'aftermath' consummated itself: frenzied Hindu mobs, driven by hate and revenge, killed nearly 10,000 innocent Sikhs across north India down to Karnataka. Four years later, Mrs Gandhi's assassins, Satwant Singh and Kehar Singh, paid the penalty for their crime by being hanged to death in Tihar jail. The killers of 10,000 Sikhs remain unpunished. The conclusion is clear: in secular India there is one law for the Hindu majority, another for Muslims, Christians and Sikhs who are in the minority.

31 October 1984: The sequence of events remains as vivid as ever. Around 11 a.m. I heard of Mrs Gandhi being shot in her house and taken to hospital. By the afternoon, I heard on the BBC that she was dead. For a couple of hours, life in Delhi came to a standstill. Then all hell broke loose—mobs yelling 'khoon ka badla khoon se lenge' (we'll avenge blood with blood) roamed the streets. Ordinary Sikhs going about their lives were waylaid and roughed up. In the evening, I saw a cloud of black smoke billowing up from Connaught Circus: Sikh-owned shops had been set on fire. An hour later, mobs were smashing up taxis owned by Sikhs right opposite my apartment. Sikh-owned shops in Khan Market were being looted. Over a hundred policemen armed with lathis lined the middle of the road and did nothing. At midnight, truckloads of men armed with cans of petrol attacked the gurdwara behind my back garden, beat up the granthi and set fire to the shrine. I was bewildered and did not know what to do. Early next morning, I rang up President Zail Singh. He would not come

to the phone. His secretary told me that the president advised me to move into the home of a Hindu friend till the trouble was over. The newly-appointed prime minister, Rajiv Gandhi, was busy receiving guests arriving for his mother's funeral; Home Minister Narasimha Rao did not budge from his office; the lieutenant governor of Delhi had no orders to put down the rioters. Seventy-two gurdwaras were torched and thousands of Sikh houses looted. The next few days, TV and radio sets were available for less than half their price.

Mid-morning, a Swedish diplomat came and took me and my wife to his home in the diplomatic enclave. My aged mother had been taken by Romesh Thapar to his home. Our family lawyer, Anant Bir Singh, who lived close to my mother, cut off his long hair and shaved his beard to avoid being recognized as a Sikh. I watched Mrs Gandhi's cremation on TV in the home of my Swedish protector. I felt like a Jew must have in Nazi Germany. I was a refugee in my own homeland because I was a Sikh.

What I found most distressing was the attitude of many of my Hindu friends. Only two couples made a point to call on me after I returned home. They were Sri S. Mulgaonkar and his wife and Arun Shourie and his wife Anita. As for the others, the less said the better. Girilal Jain, editor of *The Times of India*, rationalized the violence: the Hindu cup of patience, he wrote, had become full to the brim. N. C. Menon, who succeeded me as editor of the *Hindustan Times*, wrote of how Sikhs had 'clawed their way to prosperity' and well-nigh had it coming to them. Some spread gossip of how Sikhs had poisoned Delhi's drinking water, how they had attacked trains and slaughtered Hindu passengers. At the Gymkhana Club, where I played tennis every morning, one man said I had no right to complain after what Sikhs had done to Hindus in Punjab. At a party, another gloated, 'Khoob mazaa chakhaya' (We gave them a taste of their own medicine). Word had gone round: 'Teach the Sikhs a lesson'.

Did the Sikhs deserve to be taught a lesson? I pondered over the matter for many days and many hours and reluctantly admitted that Hindus had some justification for their anger against Sikhs. The starting point was the emergence of Jarnail Singh Bhindranwale as a leader. He used vituperative language against the Hindus. He exhorted every Sikh to kill thirty-two Hindus to solve the Hindu-Sikh problem. Anyone who opposed him was put on his hit list and some eliminated. More depressing to me was that no one spoke out openly against him. He had a wily patron in Giani Zail Singh who had him released when he was charged as an accomplice in the murder of Jagat Narain. Akali leaders supported him. Some like Badal and Barnala, who used to tie their beards to their chins, let them down in deference to his wishes. So did many Sikh civil servants. They lauded him as the saviour of the Khalsa Panth and called him 'sant'. I am proud to say I was the only one who wrote against him and attacked him as a hate-monger. I was on his hit list and continued to be on that of his followers—for fifteen long years—and was given police protection, which I never asked for.

Bhindranwale, with the tacit connivance of Akali leaders like Gurcharan Singh Tohra, turned the Golden Temple into an armed fortress of Sikh defiance. He provided the Indian government the excuse to send the army into the temple complex. I warned the government, in Parliament and through my articles, against using the army to get hold of Bhindranwale and his followers as the consequences would be grave. And so they were. Operation Blue Star was a blunder of Himalayan proportions. Bhindranwale was killed but hailed as a martyr. Over 5,000 men and women lost their lives in the exchange of fire. The Akal Takht was wrecked.

Symbolic protests did not take long coming. I was part of it; I surrendered the Padma Bhushan awarded to me. Amongst the people who condemned my action was Vinod Mehta, then editor of *The Observer*. He wrote that when it came to choosing between being an Indian or a Sikh, I had chosen to be a Sikh. I stopped contributing to his paper. I had never believed that I had to be one or the other. I was both an Indian and a Sikh and proud of being so. I might well have asked Mehta in return, 'Are you a Hindu or an Indian?' Hindus do not have to prove their nationality; only Muslims, Christians and Sikhs are required to give evidence of their patriotism.

Anti-Sikh violence gave a boost to the demand for a separate Sikh state and Khalistan-inspired terrorism in Punjab and abroad. Amongst the worst was the blowing up of Air India's *Kanishka* (23 June 1985); all its 329 passengers and crew, including over thirty

Sikhs, lost their lives. Sant Harchand Singh Longowal, who signed the Rajiv–Longowal accord (24 July 1985), was murdered while praying in a gurdwara just three weeks later. General A. S. Vaidya, who was chief of staff when Operation Blue Star took place, was gunned down in Pune in August 1986. The killings went on unabated for almost ten years during which over 25,000 were killed. Terrorists ran a parallel government in districts adjoining Pakistan, which also provided them arms training and escape routes.

The Golden Temple had again become a sanctuary for criminals. This time, Punjab police, led by K. P. S. Gill, was able to get the better of the terrorists, with the loss of only two lives, in what came to be known as Operation Black Thunder (13–18 May 1988). The terrorist movement petered out as the terrorists turned gangsters and took to extortion and robbery. The peasantry turned its back on them. About the last action of Khalistani terrorists was the murder of Chief Minister Beant Singh, who was blown up along with twelve others by a suicide bomber on 31 August 1995, at Chandigarh.

It is not surprising that with this legacy of ill-will and bloodshed a sense of alienation grew amongst the Sikhs. It was reinforced by the reluctance of successive governments at the centre to bring the perpetrators of the anti-Sikh pogrom of 31 October and 1 November 1984 to justice. A growing number of non-Sikhs have also come to the conclusion that grave injustice has been done to the Sikhs. Several non-official commissions of inquiry—including one headed by retired Supreme Court Chief Justice S. M. Sikri, comprising retired ambassadors and senior civil servants—have categorically named the guilty. However, all that the government has done is to appoint one commission of inquiry after another to look into charges of minor relevance to the issue without taking any action.

I have to concede that the attitude of the BJP government led by Atal Bihari Vajpayee and L. K. Advani towards the Sikhs has been more positive than that of the Congress, many of whose leaders were involved in the 1984 anti-Sikh violence. Some of it may be due to its alliance with the principal Sikh political party, the Akalis, led by Parkash Singh Badal. It also gives them a valid excuse to criticize the Congress leadership. Nevertheless, I welcomed the Congress Party's return to power in the centre because it also promises a fairer deal to other minorities like the Muslims and Christians. And I make no secret of my rejoicing over the choice of Manmohan Singh, the first Sikh to become prime minister of India and he in his turn selecting another Sikh, Montek Singh Ahluwalia, to head the Planning Commission.

The dark months of alienation are over; the new dawn promises blue skies and sunshine for the minorities with only one black cloud remaining to be blown away—a fair deal to families of victims of the anti-Sikh violence of 1984. It was the most horrendous crime committed on a mass scale since we became an independent nation. Its perpetrators must be punished because unpunished crimes generate more criminals.

PART III
PUNJABIS

RANJIT SINGH
(1780–1839)

Maharaja Ranjit Singh was undoubtedly the greatest son of Punjab, but he was not a handsome, anaemic, saintly character. He was a small, ugly man who loved the good things in life, liquor, good-looking men and women around him. He loved horses and leading his troops in battle. To wit Rudyard Kipling:

Four things greater than all things are
Women and horses and power and War.

While still a boy, Ranjit got smallpox, which blinded him in one eye and left his face pockmarked. Emily Eden, who was with her brother the Governor General, Lord Auckland, when they called on the maharaja, described him as 'exactly like an old mouse, with grey whiskers, one eye and a grey beard'. A legend claims that his favourite Muslim mistress, Bibi Mohran, in whose name he had a coin struck, once asked him where he was when God was distributing good looks. He replied, 'When you were asking for a comely appearance, I asked Him for power.' Before meeting him, the Governor General asked the maharaja's chief minister, Fakir Azizuddin, what his master looked like. Fakir Azizuddin gave him a diplomatic answer: 'His face has so much jalaal (dazzle) that I have never dared to look at him.'

Emily Eden wrote about Ranjit Singh's partiality for strong liquor. Dr Martin Honigberger, who prepared gunpowder for the maharaja's artillery, also prepared brandy for the royal table.

At the state banquet, Emily took care to sit on the blind-eye side of the maharaja, who poured the drinks himself in the gold goblets of the guests seated on either side of him. Every time he turned to talk to the Governor General, Emily quietly emptied her goblet on the carpet. Ranjit filled it over and over again and then turned to one of his courtiers and said in Punjabi: 'Mem taan khoob peendee hai (this white woman can hold her drink).' Once he asked a Frenchman whether it was better for the health to drink after a meal as some doctors advised or before the meal as others said. The Frenchman replied that drinking, both before and after meals, was good for one's health. The maharaja roared with happy laughter.

One aspect of Ranjit Singh's character, which made him unique amongst the Indian rulers, was that he was totally free of religious prejudice. It is said that a calligraphist who had spent the best part of his life preparing a copy of the Quran came to Lahore after having failed to sell his work to the Muslim chiefs of India. Ranjit Singh paid a fabulous price for the work. When Fakir Azizuddin praised him for his broadmindedness, the maharaja replied: 'God wanted me to look upon all religions with one eye, that is why he took away the light from the other.'

Though slaughter of kin was forbidden and many of his Hindu and European officers did not cut their hair and beards to please him, he did not impose his views on anyone. His council of ministers was dominated by the three Fakir brothers; it included Dogras and, of course, Sardars, Sandhawalias, Majithas, Attariwalas and others. Likewise, his army, trained by European officers, comprised all communities. The cavalry was largely Sikh, the artillery, commanded by General Elahi Bakhsh, largely Muslim, and the infantry, a mix of Dogras, Gorkhas, Sikhs and Muslim Najibs. His commanders on the battlefield were men like Diwan Mohkam Chand and his son, Diwan Chand, Hari Singh Nalwa and Prince Sher Singh. In short, it was a composite Punjabi fighting force that created history by reversing the tide of conquests back to the homelands of the traditional invaders—the Pathans and the Afghans.

Nothing proves Ranjit's credentials more than when it came to determining the future of the diamond Kohinoor. Instead of leaving it to one of his sons or donating it to the Harmandir, which he had renovated in marble and gold leaf, he wished it to be given to the temple of Jagannath in Puri.

It is ironic that it was the Akali Dal-BJP government of Punjab, led by Parkash Singh Badal, that took the lead in organizing the celebrations of the second centenary of his coronation some years ago. Ranjit Singh had little respect for the Akalis of his time: 'Kuj faham wa kotch andesh (of crooked minds and short-sightedness).'

BABA KHARAK SINGH
(1867–1963)

The life of Baba Kharak Singh illustrates the theme of the conflict between absolute integrity and compromise. It could be summed up in the statement that while compromise is the essence of success, uncompromising integrity is the essence of immortality. The Baba did not succeed in any worldly sense but he did win for himself a reputation for uprightness that will never die. He was known as the betaj badshah—the uncrowned emperor—of the Sikhs. The actual crown, i.e. the fruits of his endeavour went to people who were more worldly-wise and knew the art of give and take. While Kharak Singh went into the political wilderness, his younger colleagues in the Akali movement reaped a bumper harvest of political power. Master Tara Singh gained control of Sikh organizations; Giani Kartar Singh was many times a minister of the state government; Partap Singh Kairon became chief minister of East Punjab. And there were many others.

Kharak Singh's childhood was not in any way spectacular or indicative of his future career. He was born in Sialkot in 1868. His father was a contractor who made a profitable living in British army cantonments. The family were Ahluwalias by caste—a consideration of some importance even in the professedly casteless Sikh society, the majority of whom were Jat agriculturists.

The Singh Sabha which started in the 1890s was in some respects a movement of Sikh resurgence; it claimed the adherence of most educated Sikhs. The Singh Sabha stood for the teaching of Punjabi in the Gurmukhi script; for Sikh schools and colleges where the traditions of the hirsute Khalsa were instilled into young men; for resistance towards the absorptive tendencies of Hinduism; for separate electorates and privileges for the Sikhs; and above all, for loyalty towards the

British Raj. Kharak Singh's family were ardent Singh Sabhaites.

The winds of change began to blow across Punjab and assumed the violence of a gale during the First World War. The Ghadr Conspiracy of 1915 and the shooting at Jallianwala Bagh in April 1919 swept away all vestiges of loyalty towards an administration which supported butchers like General Dyer and the lieutenant governor of Punjab, Sir Michael O'Dwyer. Amongst the most powerful converts to the freedom movement was young Kharak Singh.

The massacre at Jallianwala Bagh was followed by several weeks of aerial bombings of villages, floggings without trial and other indignities; it was an anarchical 'diarchy'—a word coined by Mahatma Gandhi. The Mahatma came to Punjab and, inspired by him, a radical group of Sikhs broke away from the Singh Sabha to form the Central Sikh League. The League pledged itself to non-cooperation and soon became a part of the Indian National Congress. The moving spirit behind the League was Kharak Singh.

Kharak Singh was a devout Sikh. The misuse of Sikh shrines by mahants (priests who were as often Udasi Hindus as orthodox Sikhs) had begun to agitate the minds of the Sikhs—the most agitated person was Kharak Singh. He was amongst the pioneers of the Akali movement designed to oust these hereditary priests from the control of the gurdwaras and replace them with elected committees. The transfer of control went smoothly for some time till the flare-up at Nankana, the birthplace of Guru Nanak. At the Janamasthan (birthplace) the Udasi priest, Narain Das, hired a band of thugs and butchered in cold blood 131 Akalis who had come to take possession of the shrine.

The Nankana massacre gave a tremendous fillip to the movement. Bands of Akalis began to eject the priests and take possession of the gurdwaras. They were organized into committees under the overall control of the Shiromani Gurudwara Parbandhak Committee (SGPC) at Amritsar. The first office bearers of the SGPC were the old loyalists of the Singh Sabha. They were voted out within a few months and Kharak Singh became its president. He was also the moving spirit behind the paramilitary volunteer organization, the Shiromani Akali Dal.

The priests resisted being ejected by asking for police protection.

The authorities decided to help them and began arresting Akali volunteers. In some places, as at Guru ka Bagh near Amritsar, Akali passive resisters were subjected to savage torture. The Akali movement continued with unabated force for almost five years. Kharak Singh and thousands of other Sikhs were imprisoned over and over again. The government yielded eventually and in 1925 passed the Sikh Gurdwaras Act, handing over control of all Sikh shrines to the SGPC. This was the year of Kharak Singh's triumph. He did indeed become the uncrowned king of the Sikhs.

Immediately after winning the battle of the gurdwaras, the Akalis split into different factions. Kharak Singh led the group which aligned itself with the Congress. He was again imprisoned in the civil disobedience movement. He won undying fame for his conduct in Dera Ghazi Khan Jail. To protest against the jailers' decision to forbid Congress prisoners from wearing Gandhi caps, the Baba refused to wear anything except his kachha. He spent four bitter Punjab winters without any covering on his person. His capacity to bear suffering was truly superhuman. In the Akali and Congress agitations, the Baba was imprisoned eighteen times and spent a total of twenty years in jail.

The Baba's break with the Congress came with the Nehru Report. He felt that the Congress had been unfair to the Sikhs and not only denounced the party but also Sikhs like Master Tara Singh who did not sever their connections with the Congress.

The word 'compromise' did not exist in Kharak Singh's dictionary. He found himself isolated and out of the stream of political movements. He had to suffer the adoration of the Sikh masses who yet refused to be guided by him. He saw lesser men climb to fame and popularity and his own following dwindle to a few unscrupulous men whose only interest was to exploit his great name towards their own ends.

Baba Kharak Singh's last many years were extremely lonely. He retreated into his shell, spending many hours of the day in prayer. His closest companion was his faithful Alsatian, Badal. The dog fetched the Baba's mail and his newspapers; it fetched the servants when the master was in need; and it kept away intruders. In the heart of the capital the Baba lived in virtual vanaprastha. He died as all Indians would like to die—a dedicated sanyasi.

GIANI ZAIL SINGH
(1916–1994)

When Giani Zail Singh was sworn in as the seventh rashtrapati of India on 25 July 1980, I was rash enough to forecast that despite his modest education and inability to speak English, he would prove to be the most popular president the country had had thus far—outstripping the suave Rajendra Prasad, the scholarly S. Radhakrishnan and Zakir Hussain, garrulous V. V. Giri and Neelam Sanjiva Reddy and the all-too-pliable Fakhruddin Ali Ahmad. He started off with a bang. On Thursday, 8 July 1980, he came to the Central Hall of Parliament to bid farewell to fellow parliamentarians and announce the termination of his long association with the Congress Party. He was a few minutes late and was visibly embarrassed as Prime Minister Indira Gandhi was addressing the assemblage.

She further embarrassed him by her words of welcome: 'See, he is blushing like a bride!' So the Giani did, to the roots of his glossy black dyed beard. His farewell speech to fellow politicians was a tour de force of sentimental oratory the like of which is rarely heard these days. He ended with a reference to Mrs Gandhi's quip about his blushing, admitting that he felt like an Indian bride taking leave of her parents, brothers and sisters when every member of the family is in tears. 'You have decided to retire me from politics; however, mine will be a kind of a shaahee retirement,' he concluded.

His first few months as rashtrapati were roses, roses all the way. Wherever he went, he was welcomed by mammoth crowds. He regaled them with rustic anecdotes, Urdu couplets, Persian and Punjabi poetry, quotations from sacred Sanskrit texts, the Quran and the Granth Sahib. Here at last was a 'people's rashtrapati', earthy, one who could talk on the same level to the peasant and the artisan; enter into a dialogue with the pandit, the maulvi and the granthi. The only class with which he neither tried nor was capable of making an equation was the westernized woggery. They cracked their Sardarji jokes at his expense at their cocktail parties. He often exposed himself to their jibes as he did when criticizing the Darwinian theory of our descent from the apes: 'How could the Buddha be a progeny of a monkey?' he asked naively.

But few wags dared to take him on in public because they knew they could not hope to match him in witty repartee. He ignored their existence.

The one thing that had irked the sophisticated sections of society was his exaggerated deference to the 'royal family'. He said he would be willing to sweep the floor if Mrs Gandhi so desired and acknowledged the then seeming heir-apparent, Sanjay, as his rehnuma (guide). Few people realized that darbardari (flattery) was deeply ingrained in his psyche as he was born and brought up in the courtly atmosphere of Faridkot Raj where only sycophancy and cunning ensured survival.

Within a few months, things began to go awry. It was his own community which had earlier lauded his elevation as the first Sikh rashtrapati that began to deride him. The Akalis launched their 'dharma yuddha morcha' against the government. The Giani mocked them: 'Akali, akal ke khalee (Akalis are empty headed)'. They retaliated by describing him as a sarkari Sikh and the prime minister's rubber stamp. Akali demonstrations against the ninth Asiad gave Bhajan Lal's Haryana constabulary freedom to harass all Sikhs coming to Delhi by rail and road. For the first time in the history of independent India, Sikhs came to be discriminated against. It was ironic that this should have started when a Sikh presided over the country. His stock amongst the Sikh community began to decline. Then events overtook him with rapid succession—Operation Blue Star was followed by Operation Woodrose to comb the Punjab countryside for terrorists.

Gianiji had been kept in the dark about Blue Star but the Sikhs held him responsible for it. High priests of the Takhts summoned him to explain why he should not be declared a tankhaiya. In many gurdwaras posters with his pictures were laid out on the floor at the entrance for worshippers to tread on. His TV appearance visiting the

Harmandir Sahib after the carnage wearing a rose in his sherwani caused a wave of resentment. He was virtually written off by his community. Then came the assassination of Mrs Indira Gandhi followed by the massacre of Sikhs in towns and cities of northern India. Being a Sikh, the Giani had to suffer the odium with which Hindus began to regard his community.

Hardly had the country returned to normalcy and the Giani regained his equipoise, than the new prime minister, Rajiv Gandhi, began to exhibit boorishness unbecoming of a young man of his lineage towards an elder to whom he initially owed his position. The Giani felt isolated and unwanted. I was pretty certain that he was looking for a suitable opportunity to resign and to go out of the Rashtrapati Bhavan with the same fanfare with which he had entered it. I was wrong. He stepped out of his mansion not with the proverbial bang, but not with a whimper either.

In the last six months, he gave Rajiv Gandhi and his advisers a taste of their own medicine and many sleepless nights. What is more, if they had any illusions of making up for lost sleep after Gianiji quit Rashtrapati Bhavan, they were in for a nasty surprise. Unlike his predecessors, who disappeared into pastoral oblivion after their retirement, Gianiji was a retired president living in the capital and determined to level his score with the prime minister. I foresaw Gianiji becoming the patron saint of those disenchanted with the regime.

Although he did not fulfil my prophecy of being the most popular president of the republic, he will undoubtedly go down in the pages of history as the most talked about president of the Indian republic.

What was there in this man of humble origins and little academic learning that helped him overcome one obstacle after another and pedestal himself to triumph, to reach the pinnacle of aspiration and become the head of state? I will let incidents in his life speak for him.

Zail Singh was an active worker of Praja Mandal of the erstwhile Faridkot state. The raja had personally ordered him to be jailed. When India became independent and Faridkot was merged into the Patiala and East Punjab States Union (PEPSU), the central government was looking for suitable men to run the new state. Sardar Vallabhbhai Patel summoned Zail Singh. Zail Singh did not have the money to buy a third-class return ticket from Faridkot to Delhi and had to ask friends for a loan. In Delhi, he stayed in Gurdwara Sis Ganj. He did not have money to hire a tonga to take him to Sardar Patel's residence at five in the morning. He walked the entire four miles and was late for his appointment. Sardar Patel's daughter brusquely dismissed him. It was the kindly secretary, V. Shankar, who let him see the deputy prime minister. Zail Singh was told that he was being made minister of state in PEPSU. He walked back to the railway station to return to Faridkot. He never looked back. He did not forget his humble origins nor let power go to his head.

Success was to him a gift given by the Great Guru, not something owed to him by virtue of his abilities.

One of his favourite couplets warns one of the dangers of hubris:

Jin mein ho jaata hai andaz-e-khudaee paida
Hum ne dekha hai voh butt toot jaate hain.

Mortals who allow notions of divinity to germinate in them
We have seen those idols shattered and come to grief.

There is not even a suspicion of arrogance or self-esteem in this man. Besides humility, his faith in religion taught him to be honest and truthful. He is one of the breed of politicians, now almost extinct, who though handling vast sums of money never feathered his own nest nor those of his relatives. He owns no house, flat or tract of land except the little he inherited.

Nobody has ever accused him of telling a lie. As a junior minister, Zail Singh set about assiduously cultivating the support of the lower and discriminated castes. He is a Ramgarhia (carpenter). Punjab has always been dominated by Jat and Sikh politics constipated with caste considerations. Zail Singh broke the Jat hegemony over the state and successfully mocked Akali pretensions of being thekedars (monopolists) of the Khalsa Panth. He was able to convince the Sikhs that he was a better Sikh than all the Akali leaders put together. His speeches were always full of quotations from the Gurbani and episodes from Sikh history. No other politician, either from the Akali party or the Congress, could build this kind of Gursikh image for himself as did the Giani. By the time he made his presence felt in the state, a precedent had been established that the chief minister of Punjab should be a Sikh. There was no better Sikh than Giani Zail Singh to fill the role. Zail Singh's six-year tenure as the chief minister was perhaps the most peaceful and prosperous the state has ever seen. They were the years of the Green Revolution. They were also the years without morchas, bandhs or strikes. The Giani was able to rekindle pride in Punjabiyat. From England he acquired the mortal remains of Madan Lal Dhingra who had been hanged for the murder of Curzon Wyllie, and of Udham Singh, hanged for the murder of Sir Michael O'Dwyer, governor of Punjab at the time of Jallianwala Bagh, and he raised martyrs' memorials over them. He sought out the long-forgotten and ailing mother of Bhagat Singh, gave her a handsome grant and had her honoured as Punjab Mata—Mother of Punjab. The road connecting Anandpur to Fatehgarh was named Guru Gobind Singh Marg; horses believed to be descendants of the Guru's steed were taken along the marg for the populace to see and marvel at.

A new township, Baba Ajit Singh Nagar, was named after the Guru's eldest son. Massive keertan darbars were organized all over the state. In his eagerness to wrest the Akali monopoly over the affairs of the Khalsa Panth, he unwittingly set in motion a Sikh revivalism which turned into fundamentalism under Jarnail Singh Bhindranwale.

Gianiji could not have foreseen this development, much less wished it, because his relations with Punjabi Hindus including the somewhat anti-Sikh Mahasha press of Jalandhar, remained extremely cordial. And if gossip is to be believed, more than cordial with the smaller Muslim community. Giani Zail Singh achieved the incredible: he had no enemies. Besides being a Punjabi paradigm of a dostaan da dost (of friends the friendliest) he had the knack of winning over detractors. Even in the heyday of his power as chief minister and home minister, he never tried to settle scores with people who had persecuted or humiliated him. He won them over by granting them favours and making them ashamed of themselves. If there was anything he could do for anyone, he never hesitated to do it. He had an incredibly good memory for names and faces. He was able to gain friends by simply recognizing people he had met briefly.

During the Emergency, while he had put many people in jail, he went to see them. He sent a wedding gift to P. S. Badal's daughter when her father was in prison and went to receive the baraat at the house of a friend's daughter in Kalka when her father was locked up. If he heard a friend was sick he would find time to visit him in hospital and quietly slip a bundle of currency notes under his pillow. Virtually the only man he was unable to win over was Darbara Singh who succeeded him as chief minister of Punjab.

To describe Gianiji as a far-sighted statesman would be an exaggeration; to describe him as a cunning politician would be grossly unfair because the stock-in-trade of a cunning politician is the ability to tell a blatant lie. And the one thing no one can accuse Gianiji of is falsehood. He is best described as a shrewd judge of men and events.

After Mrs Gandhi's murder, there were many claimants to the prime ministership. Oddly enough, one of the senior-most civil servants at the time and later a confidant of the present prime minister even suggested to Gianiji that he take over the prime ministership himself. Sensing the anti-Sikh climate of the day, it was Gianiji who brushed aside this inane suggestion and decided to offer it to Rajiv Gandhi in the belief that as the descendant of Nehru and Indira Gandhi, he would be best suited to hold the country together.

And when the Opposition tried to put him up for a second term and Congress dissidents assured him of a substantial vote from the Congress Party, he carefully weighed his prospects before turning it down. He was not a gambler; he played to win. It was the same when pressure was brought on him to dismiss the prime minister or permit his prosecution on charges of corruption. Gianiji had little to lose and he could have made things very hot for Rajiv Gandhi. He refused to succumb to temptation, teaching Rajiv a lesson for his bad behaviour, because he felt that the nation's future was paramount and India was more important than Rajiv Gandhi or Zail Singh.

He has often quoted a couplet to the effect that while he put a rose in the palms of Rajiv Gandhi, Rajiv took a stone to hurt him. There is an equally apt couplet for him to mull over in his days of retirement:

Zakhmee hue jo hont to mahsoos yeh hua
Chooma tha maine phool ko deevanagi ke sath.

It was the bruises on my lips that made me comprehend
With what thoughtlessness I had kissed the rose.

P. C. LAL
(1916–1982)

There is a Hindustani saying that men of destiny have signs of greatness even in their infancy. No one who knew Pratap Lal in school and college spotted any such telltale signs indicating the heights to which he would rise. We became friends at Modern School when we were only five years old. Ten years later, we exchanged turbans to become dharambhais—brothers in faith. There was nothing dharmic about my intentions; though only fifteen, I was besotted with Pratap's sister, Roma, who was two years older than me. She was the heart-throb of my generation.

The Lals were a mixed Punjabi-Bengali family. Pratap's father Rai Bahadur Basant Lal, assistant commissioner of income tax, was a Punjabi, his mother was a Bengali Sarkar who spoke Punjabi fluently. In their home they spoke four languages with equal fluency: English, Hindustani, Bengali and Punjabi. They were Brahmos, more liberal in their views than most Indian families of Delhi.

The outbreak of war in 1939 rescued Pratap Lal from what might well have been an undistinguished career at the Bar. He promptly threw away his law books and joined the air force. Being familiar with the workings of aircraft, he had no problem rising rapidly up the ranks. And displayed yet another unknown characteristic: bravery.

He flew dive bombers supporting General W. J. Slim's drive against the Japanese in Burma. He was awarded the Distinguished Flying Cross. When Independence came he held the rank of squadron leader. He was chosen for an advanced course in Andover and was the first pilot of the Indian Air Force to fly faster than the speed of sound.

In 1966, he was made managing director of the Hindustan Aeronautics Limited factory at Bangalore.

My wife and I spent some days with him and his wife Ela (Hashi). They were an abstemious couple. He did not smoke or drink. We had to extort our quota of Scotch from him every evening. He was also very prudish. No talk of nudity or sex. No dirty jokes.

The air operations in the 1971 war against Pakistan were masterminded by Lal. It was his strategy that knocked out the teeth of the Pakistani Air Force in Bangladesh. Within a few hours of the declaration of the war, the Dacca and Chittagong airstrips were rendered unserviceable; the Pakistani Air Force mess next to the Dacca airport was knocked out by a direct hit and the governor cowed to submission by a hail of bullets fired into the windows of his residence. Another trait that none of his contemporaries had suspected in Lal was efficiency and hard work. The way he streamlined the functioning of Air India and Indian Airlines, refusing doggedly to give in to arm-twisting by the pilots' union, earned him a deserved reputation as a first-class administrator.

Lal was a magnanimous man. He was removed from his post of Chairman of Air India and Indian Airlines by Sanjay Gandhi and took a job with the Tatas. When Sanjay fell from power and most people avoided meeting members of the Gandhi family, I had to go to Calcutta to appear as a co-accused with Maneka Gandhi in a case against *Surya*. I was staying with the Lals; Maneka with Kamal Nath. 'The Lals must hate us,' I recall Maneka telling me. Lal hated no one. It was Hashi who invited Maneka over to their house and instead of showing any resentment against what had been done to them, treated her with great courtesy and affection.

Pratap died in London on 13 August 1982. I was present at his cremation the next day in the Delhi electric crematorium. So ended a friendship that had lasted over half a century. Shakespeare's lines from *Julius Caesar* are the most fitting tribute I could pay to my departed friend:

His life was gentle.
And the elements so mixed in him
That nature itself would stand up and say
to all the world: This was a Man.

MANZUR QADIR
(1913–1974)

My closest friend of many years lay dying; I could not go to his bedside. His wife and children were only an hour and a half's flight from me; I could not go to see them. I could not ring them up nor write to them. And when he died, I was not there to comfort them. They are Pakistani, I am Indian. What kind of neighbours are we? What right have we to call ourselves civilized?

I had missed the news in the morning paper. When a friend rang me up and said, 'Your old friend is gone,' the blood in my veins froze. I picked up the paper from the wastepaper basket and saw it in black and white. Manzur Qadir was dead. At the time he was dying in London, I was drinking and listening to Vividh Bharati in Bombay. And when he was being laid to rest in the family graveyard at Lahore, I was wringing my hands in despair in Colaba. He was Pakistani, I am Indian.

It is believed that when a person is dying, all the events of his life flash before his mind's eye. I must have occupied many precious seconds of Manzur Qadir's dying thoughts as he also regarded me as his closest friend. I spent the whole morning thinking of how we met and why I was drawn close to him. At our first meeting thirty years ago we had talked about death. I had quoted lines from the last letter his wife Asghari's brother had written to his father, Mian Fazl-i-Husain:

I am working by candlelight,
It flickers, it's gone.

Manzur Qadir was a man of contradictions. He showed little promise as a student; he became the most outstanding lawyer of Pakistan. Next to law, his favourite reading was the Old Testament and the Quran. Nevertheless he remained an agnostic to the very last. He was an uncommonly good poet and wrote some of the wittiest, bawdiest verse known in the Urdu language. At the same time he was extremely conservative, correct in his speech and deportment. Although born a Punjabi he rarely spoke the language and preferred to converse in Hindustani, which he did with uncommon elegance. He was long-winded but never a bore; a teetotaller who effervesced like vintage champagne.

The dominant traits of his character were kindliness—he never said a hurtful word about anyone—and integrity which surpassed belief. He made upwards of Rs 50,000 a month; income tax authorities were constantly refunding tax he had paid in excess. He did not give a tinker's cuss about money. It was commonly said, 'God may lie, but not Manzur Qadir.' Though godless he had more goodness in him than a clutch of saints.

The respect and admiration he commanded amongst his friends was unparalleled. Some years after Partition, a group of us were discussing G. D. Khosla's *Stern Reckoning*. The book, as the title signifies, justified the killings that took place in East Punjab in the wake of Partition as legitimate retribution. We were going for Khosla's partisan approach; he and his wife were arguing back. Suddenly a friend asked Khosla, 'Would you present a copy of this book to Manzur?' Khosla pondered for a while and replied, 'No, not to him.' That ended the argument. We came to judge the right or wrong of our actions by how Manzur Qadir would react. He was the human touchstone of our moral pretensions.

Manzur Qadir had no interest in politics and seldom bothered to read newspapers. His ignorance of world affairs was abysmal. Once in London we happened to see a newsreel of Dr Sun Yat Sen. He asked me who this Sen was. When I expressed my amazement at his lack of information, he retorted testily: 'Hoga koee sala Bangali daktar.' Later in the evening, when I narrated the incident to his daughter Shireen, she chided her father. He made me swear I wouldn't tell anyone about it. I didn't till I read in the papers that President Ayub Khan had made him foreign minister of Pakistan. I sent him a telegram of congratulations, 'Greetings from Dr Sun Yat Sen, the Bengali doctor.'

I spent a short holiday with him when he was foreign minister. I stayed as a guest in my own home. (I had put him in possession of it when I left Lahore in August 1947. He not only saved the life of my Sikh servants, whom he brought to the Indian border at night at considerable risk to his life, but sent back every book in my library, every item of furniture and even the remaining liquor in my drinks cabinet.) He told me how he had become foreign minister. He had criticized Ayub Khan's dictatorship at a meeting. That evening an army jeep came to fetch him. Believing that he was being arrested he said goodbye to his family. He was driven to the president's residence.

Said Ayub Khan: 'It is no good criticizing me and my government unless you are willing to take responsibility for what you say.' Manzur Qadir returned home as foreign minister.

True to his character, Manzur never canvassed for any job nor showed the slightest eagerness to hold on to power. He strove with none, for none was worth his strife. He allowed himself to be outmanoeuvred by unscrupulous politicians. After four years as foreign minister, during which he made a desperate bid to improve relations with India, he quit the job with no regrets. He was forced to become chief justice and, when he desired to throw that up, persuaded to take up briefs on behalf of the government. He was engaged as government counsel in all the important conspiracy cases and represented his country before international tribunals; whether it was Iskander Mirza or Ayub Khan, Yahya Khan or Bhutto, no ruler of Pakistan could do without Manzur Qadir.

Last year I spent a day with him in Nathiagali near Murree. He was a very sick man afflicted with phlebitis. But for old times' sake, he drove down to Islamabad to pick me up and drove me back the next evening. I saw for myself the affection and esteem with which he was held by everyone from General Tikka Khan down to the humblest tradesman in the bazaar. It was a continuous shaking of hands and salaam alaikums.

He bore the pain of his illness with incredible courage and without the slightest attempt to find false props offered by religion. He knew he had a short time to go but had no fear of death. I forget the Urdu couplet he used to quote but it was very much like Charles Wesley's lines:

If I must die, I will encounter darkness as a bride and hug
it in my arms.
When summoned hence to thine eternal sleep, oh, mayest

thou smile while all round thee weep.

At our final farewell, the tears were in my eyes, not in his. An English friend kept me informed of his deteriorating state of health in the London hospital. Apparently, she too was not with him when the end came. Tributes to such a man as Manzur Qadir can only be written in tears which leave no stain on paper. He shall be forever honoured and forever mourned. Robert Browning's lines were meant for a man like him:

We that had loved him so, followed him, honoured him,
Lived in his mild and magnificent eye,
Learned his great language, caught his clear accents,
Made him our pattern to live and to die.

Manzur Qadir died on 12 October 1974.

Whenever I visit Lahore, one of my top assignments is to visit his grave, strew rose petals on it, recite the fateha and shed some tears.

Manzur's son, Basharat, had chosen Allama Iqbal's lines for his father's epitaph:

Main to jaltee hoon ke muzmir meri fitrat main soze
Tu ferozaan hai keh parvano se ho sauda tera.

I burn because it is in my nature to burn and give light.
You burn and give light to enter into a contract with the moth.

Basharat transposed the lines to form a more fitting tribute to his father:

I burn because it is in my nature to do so
Moths are drawn to you because with warmth you glow.

NANAK SINGH
(1922–2001)

The most flamboyant character I have ever met in my long life was Nanak Singh who died in mid-February just short of turning eighty. Not only did he move from a hovel to a three-storeyed marble mansion, from plying a cycle-rickshaw to riding a chauffeur-driven Mercedes Benz, from a pauper to becoming a multi-millionaire, he was also a lavish spender the like of which I have never met. A lover of beautiful women, and lover of Urdu poetry, he was also illiterate.

He descended on me one Diwali morning some ten years ago. My servant refused to let him in because he had not made an appointment. A few minutes later he rang me up from nearby Khan Market to say who he was and did not think he needed an appointment to see anyone on Diwali. And added, 'I am told you don't believe in God; I want to tell you I have met God face to face.' I apologized and asked him to come over. He was back in a couple of minutes. I opened the door for him. Following him was his chauffeur carrying a huge basket full of dry fruit, two watermelons (garma and sarda from Kabul) and two bottles of premium scotch; an wholly unexpected bonanza from a total stranger.

After he was seated, I asked him about his meeting with God. He replied curtly, 'Not today. You've spoilt my mood by turning me back. I'll tell you about Him another day.'

Thereafter Nanak Singh came to see me many times—after making an appointment. Nanak Milk was delivered at my doorstep free of charge every day. Despite my protests, he gave hundred-rupee notes to my servants. He told me about his past but evaded my direct questions about his dialogue with the Almighty. He came from a Hindu-Sikh family (his brothers were Hindus) of very modest means, living in a small village in Montgomery district (now Sahiwal) in Pakistan. One Bakr Id day he saw a butcher leading a young cow to slaughter as sacrifice. He was overcome with compassion, ran to his uncles and aunts and begged them to lend him money. He paid the butcher double the price of the cow and saved its life. He was hauled up before the All-Muslim Panchayat of the village and asked to explain his conduct. He pleaded guilty and said, 'Raham aa gayaa, aap bhee raham karo'. The panchayat forgave him. Nanak Singh explained his success in the milk business to the blessings of the Gau Mata whose life he had saved.

On the partition of the country, the family first settled in Amritsar. He plied a cycle-rickshaw and sold milk. The milk business prospered. He got a contract to supply milk to the army depot in Amritsar. He got more contracts from other army establishments. He moved to Delhi and set up chilling plants and acquired a fleet of milk tankers. During the 1971 Indo-Pak War over the liberation of Bangladesh, his tankers kept our jawans fighting on the front. He supplied milk to them. He became the single largest milk supplier of India. And a multi-millionaire. He expanded his business to producing country-liquor of good quality. And became a billionaire.

Nanak Singh liked the company of beautiful women. For his sons, he chose brides—the prettiest he could find from Sikh families of modest means. Once he invited me to bring all the beautiful women I knew to his home for dinner. I took five: Kamana Prasad, Sadia Dehlavi (and her husband Raza), Reeta Devi Verma, my wife and daughter. He ordered his daughters-in-law to be attired in their best sarees and jewellery: he was a dictator prone to order everyone around. Before we sat down to dinner, he ordered all of us to come out to his entrance gate. There were more than ten beggars awaiting him. He had parcels of warm clothing and blankets which he made us distribute among them. This was his daily routine: before he sat down to his evening meal; he gave dasvandh (one-tenth of one's income) prescribed by Sikh tradition.

His youngest son's wedding was the most lavish I have ever attended. Instead of an invitation card, there was a sandal-wood music box. As you opened it, you heard Bismillah Khan's music on the shehnai. Then Nanak Singh's voice inviting you to his son's nuptials in the most florid Urdu. The music box must have cost at least Rs 5000. The reception was on the lawn behind Ashoka Hotel. It was done up like the Taj Mahal. With me was Maya Ray (S. S. Ray's wife). Everyone who mattered in Delhi was there. Crates of French champagne were opened and guests squirted with expensive nectar. Nanak Singh was like a boy playing Holi. Famous qawwals, including Shakila Bano Bhopali, entertained the guests.

Nanak Singh had a mechanical bent of mind. Apart from designing his own electronically operated garage doors, he had designed a conveyor belt which on the press of a button brought your chosen brand of whisky from the shelf to the dining table where you were seated. Though he was not able to read or write, he often came to consult me on some petition or the other drafted by his lawyer. He would put his finger on a particular paragraph and ask me to read it: 'There is something missing here,' he would say. He was always right.

Much as I tried I could not pin down Nanak Singh to tell me of his encounter with God. He would put me off by evasive replies: 'Is not my life proof enough that there is God: how else could a pauper become what I am today, hain?'

A few years later, Nanak Singh went into deep depression. He was flown to the USA for treatment. At his son's behest, I rang him in hospital. I tried to cheer him up. 'What happened to your God? Isn't He looking after you?' He was in no mood for jesting and just moaned, 'I don't know why this is happening to me.' By the time he came back, he was beyond communication.

BHAGAT PURAN SINGH
(1904–1992)

Sometime in 1980, I happened to be addressing a convocation of the Khalsa College in Amritsar. I noticed an old man with a scraggy long beard, an untidy white turban wrapped around his head, dressed in khadi kurta-pyjama, engrossed in taking notes on what I was saying. I could not take my eyes off him. He disappeared as soon as the convocation was over. Later, I asked the principal of the college, who was sharing the dais with me, about the old man in the front row. 'You don't know him?' he asked in surprise. 'That was Bhagat Singh of the Pingalwara.'

'What was he writing while the speeches were going on?' I asked.

'He always does that,' replied the principal. 'If he hears anything worthwhile, he puts it in his newspaper published in Punjabi and English. In the Pingalwara, he has his own printing press.'

Bhagat Puran Singh had become a household name long before I saw him. On a subsequent visit to Amritsar, I noticed small, black tin boxes, with the word Pingalwara written in white on them, in different parts of the city. These had a slit on top, through which people could put in money. I learnt that Bhagat Puran Singh was to be seen on the steps of the Golden Temple as well, holding out the hem of his kurta for people to drop alms for his home for destitutes. It had also become a practice in many families to send money to the Pingalwara when there was a wedding in the house or in memory of a deceased family member. Neither the Punjab government nor the municipality gave him any financial assistance; it was only the people who gave him just enough to feed, clothe and render medical assistance to over 800 sick men, women and children abandoned by their families.

I was intrigued and determined to meet him. From Delhi I wrote to him seeking an appointment to visit the Pingalwara and talk to him. I got a reply in Gurmukhi, written in his own hand, asking me to come as soon as I could. Three days later, I was back in Amritsar. I took a taxi from the railway station and arrived at the Pingalwara.

The first thing Bhagatji asked me was: 'How did you come here?'

'By train from Delhi, then by cab from the station,' I replied, somewhat bewildered by the question. Maybe he thought I had flown in.

'You should have come by tonga or on a bicycle,' he said quite firmly.

'Where would I find a bicycle on hire at the railway station? And a tonga would have taken more than an hour to get here,' I protested.

Bhagatji gave me a dressing down: 'Do you know how much poisonous gas a motor car emits and fouls the air?' He then proceeded to give me a long lecture on global warming and what it would do to human and animal life, forests and vegetation. He thrust some sheets of his newsletter in my hand, commanding me: 'Read this, and this, and this.'

Clearly, he was somewhat of a crackpot. I love crackpots.

I went around the Pingalwara. It did not answer the requirements of modern hygiene. People were lying on charpoys with flies buzzing around. Lavatory stench, mixed with the smell of phenyl and food being cooked, pervaded the air. Volunteers scurried around, doing the best they could. It was evident that there was shortage of everything—food, clothes, medicines, staff. How much could one man do to help 800 people?

I made a nominal donation, gathered all the printed material Bhagatji gave me and retuned to Delhi.

Back home, I wrote in my columns about Bhagatji's dedicated service and the odds he was facing. I wrote to the Punjab chief minister and whomever else I could think of. The response was heartening. More money began to flow into the Pingalwara.

Thereafter, whenever Bhagatji came to Delhi, he dropped in to see me. I did not chide him for coming in a taxi but made a token offering, which he accepted without counting the notes. A receipt followed some days later.

Bhagatji's work began to receive wider recognition. People began to make donations on a regular basis. Conditions in the Pingalwara improved and its activities expanded. No discrimination was ever made on grounds of religion or caste: the inmates included Hindus, Sikhs and Muslims; there were Brahmins, Kshatriyas, Vaishyas, Shudras and Harijans. Suffering knows no caste.

The last time I met Bhagatji was a few weeks after Operation Blue Star, which had taken a heavy toll of lives and caused extensive damage to sacred property. My reaction was immediate. Within twenty-four hours of the army assault on the Golden Temple, I had returned my Padma Bhushan to President Giani Zail Singh as a mark of protest. Bhagatji asked me if he should do the same with the Padma Shri he had been awarded in 1979; a week later, he relinquished the honour bestowed on him.

When Bhagatji died, I paid a tearful tribute to him in my columns. A few years later, I persuaded my brothers and sister to make a substantial donation on behalf of the Sir Shobha Singh Charitable Trust to the Pingalwara. It was graciously accepted by Dr Inderjit Kaur, who had taken over its management. Some months later, Dr Manmohan Singh, then minister of finance, accompanied our family to Amritsar to inaugurate a new block for patients in the Pingalwara.

It was impossible to meet Bhagatji and not feel inspired to contribute towards his mission in some manner, however modest— and his legacy of dedicated service to suffering humanity must be kept alive for generations to come. In living memory, Punjab has not produced as great a man as Bhagat Puran Singh.

VEERAN BAI
(c.1899-1985)

Of my parents, I felt more relaxed with my mother than with my father. None of her children were as scared of her as we were of our father. When we were small, she often threatened to slap us, but it never went beyond raising her hand and threatening 'maaraan chaata?' Nothing followed. She was frail, short, with little confidence in herself. Whatever little she may have had as a girl was squashed by her overbearing husband who would not trust her to run her home. He even prepared menus for his dinner parties—they hardly ever varied from tomato soup, fish, chicken, pilaf, followed by pudding— and he kept all the accounts except the dhobi's. There were other reasons for her willing subservience to her husband—her father and two brothers were in our employment; of her three sisters' husbands, two depended on my father's patronage. She had never been to school and only learned Gurmukhi to be able to write letters and read the headlines of Punjabi newspapers. She didn't waste time on books and preferred to gossip with her sisters and maidservant, Bhajno, who was an inveterate carrier of tales against her sons' wives. However, when I was abroad I got more news from the few lines she wrote to me in Gurmukhi than the two pages of typescript my father dictated to his secretary. He wrote about the government, political wrangling and the budget; she wrote about births, liaisons, marriages and deaths. She often grumbled that she could not read or write English. Despite the instructors my father employed to teach her the language, she stubbornly refused to go beyond 'yes, no, good morning, good night, goodbye and thank you'.

When the Punjabi translation of my novel *Train to Pakistan* was published, I gave her the first copy. I did not expect her to read it.

When I went to see her the next morning, my father told me that she had been reading the novel late into the night and was down with a severe headache. I went to her bedroom. She was lying covered from head to foot in her shawl. I shook her by the shoulder and asked how she was feeling. She peeped out of the shawl with one eye and made a one-word comment: 'Beysharam!' (shameless creature).

My mother was something of a hypochondriac. The only thing she really suffered from were migraine headaches. The attacks could be so severe that she had to stay in bed for two days and only felt better after she had thrown up a few times. But whenever she caught a cold she was sure it was her last moment. Whenever she felt a pain in any part of her body she was sure it was cancer. She had heard that cancer was incurable. Therefore what she had could be nothing except cancer. When my father died in his ninetieth year, she was in her eighties and in good health. Instead of being shattered by his going, as everyone expected, she came into her own as a very domineering materfamilias. Nobody dared to address her except as Lady Sobha Singh. Like Queen Victoria, she held court every day. At eleven she presided over the mid-morning coffee session; in the evening, over drinks and dinner. I persuaded her to have a little alcohol in the evenings. At first she consumed it surreptitiously. When bearers came round with tray loads of soft drinks for the ladies at parties she would tell them that her son was bringing her orange juice. I initially spiked her glass with a little gin, and then I introduced her to Scotch. Again she made a mild protest. 'What will people say! An old, illiterate woman from a village drinking whisky?' She began to like her sundowner and became discerning enough to tell good Scotch from bad desi.

In her ninetieth year she began to sense that she did not have very much longer to live. She never said anything about it but started giving things away. My father's sweaters, his ebony walking stick with a silver knob, and his gold watch came to me; jewellery and a gold watch went to my sister; jewellery, watches, gold pens, gold buttons, and sovereigns were distributed amongst sons, daughters-in-law and their progeny. There was seldom a morning when I went to see her when she did not give me a shirt, a pair of socks or shoes that my father had worn. We knew that she meant to give these things away with her own hands.

Without there being anything specifically wrong with her, she began to wither away. Dr I. P. S. Kalra, who was married to my cousin, also a doctor, came to see her twice a day to take her blood pressure and temperature. She began to spend a longer time in bed. My sister slept in her bedroom to help her go to the bathroom. Then a night maid was hired to clean, sponge and help change her clothes. Her appearances at coffee sessions became rarer and rarer. But even when half conscious, she would send for her servant, Haria, and mumble 'Coffee'. He would assure her that visitors were being served coffee. Many times my telephone rang to tell me that she was sinking. We would hurry over. Dr Kalra would be there giving her a shot of something or the other. She then rallied round and we returned to our homes. One evening, when all her children, grandchildren and a number of great-grandchildren were there, she went into a coma from which she never recovered.

We spent many hours of many days sitting by her supine body, assured by the rise and fall of her sheet that she was still alive. More than once we asked Dr Kalra not to persist in injecting her with life-saving drugs and let her go in peace. He refused to listen to us and said that he was determined to keep her alive for as long as he could. Back in my flat, I dreaded the ringing telephone. The final call came on the afternoon of 9 March 1985. It was my sister's anguished voice crying, 'She's gone.'

By the time we got to her she looked peacefully asleep. Beside her pillow, incense spiralled upwards to the ceiling. My elder brother sat by her bedside reading out from a small prayer book. Others embraced each other in tears and sat in chairs in the garden, only to break down again and again as people came to condole with them. As in earlier happenings in the family, it was my younger brother, Brigadier Gurbux Singh, who took control of the situation. He made me draft the obituary notice, corrected it and sent it off to all the Delhi papers. He fixed the time of her cremation and the day the Akhand Path would commence and terminate with bhog and kirtan. He ordered us to return to our homes for the night. He, his wife and my sister would stay with the body. My elder brother sat by her making the japs over and over again throughout the night, as he had done years earlier by our father's body.

The next morning we took our mother's body to the same electric crematorium where we had earlier taken our father and uncle. My brother, Gurbux, took her ashes to Haridwar as he had our father's ashes and those of my grandmother, to be immersed in the Ganga. Thus ended the days of Veeran Bai, Lady Sobha Singh, my mother.

ACKNOWLEDGEMENTS

Many of the essays that appear in this volume are versions of pieces that first appeared in *Yojana, New Delhi,* the *Hindustan Times, Tribune, Illustrated Weekly of India, Statesman* and *Times of India,* to name a few of the publications that Khushwant Singh contributed to. As the majority of the pieces were taken from typescripts in the possession of the author's estate, it has been difficult to accurately source the name of the publication in which the pieces first appeared. All the essays in the book have been used with permission from the author's estate. Every effort has been made to trace copyright holders and obtain permission to reproduce copyright material included in the book. In the event of any inadvertent omission, the publisher should be informed and formal acknowledgement will be included in all future editions of this book.